Can I Write Off My RV?

WHAT EVERY RVER SHOULD KNOW ABOUT TAXES

George M. Montgomery, EA

Business And Tax Planning
Mesa, AZ

Business And Tax Planning
300 S Val Vista Drive, #118
Mesa, AZ 85204-1918
www.BusinessAndTaxPlanning.com

Ordering Information:
Quantity sales. Special discounts are available on quantity
purchases by corporations, associations, and others. For de-
tails, contact the "Special Sales Department" at the address
above.

Can I Write Off My RV?/ George M Montgomery. —1st ed.
ISBN978-0-9910271-0-1

Table of Contents

1 Introduction & How To Read This Book   1

2 What Is My Background?   9

3 What Is Your Domicile?   33

4 What Expenses May I Take?   47

5 Can I Deduct The RV?   63

6 Are You An Employee Or Contractor?   73

7 Can I Voluntee?   79

8 Which Business Entity?   83

9 What Records Do I Keep?   89

10 Need To File Multi-State Tax Returns?   107

11 Where & How Do Are They Deducted?   113

12 Do You Have A Business Or Hobby?   119

13 Example Of A Part-Timer With A Home Base &
High Itemized Deductions?   125

14 Example of Part-timer With Home Base and
StandardDeduction   129

15 Example of Full-timer With Itemized
Deductions   133

16 Example of Full-timer With Standard
Deductions   137

<u>17</u> Example of Self Employed Full-timer With
Standard Deductions   145

<u>18</u> Summary: From My Point Of View   151

Appendix   161

Resources   170

Index   173

This book is dedicated to the many RVers I have met over the last 18 years. Most have been Escapees, some were Boomers, and many were Workampers. I have learned a lot from each of them about caring for and living in an RV and the problems that we all faced as we worked seasonally while living in our RVs.

Favorite Quotations

On Taxes:

"Any one may so arrange his affairs that his taxes
shall be as low as possible; he is not bound to choose
that pattern which will best pay the Treasury; there is
not even a patriotic duty to increase one's taxes."
-- Justice Billings Judge Learned Hand in rendering
his decision regarding a matter before the US Court
of Appeals. *Helvering v. Gregory*, 69 F.2d 809,
810-11 (2d Cir. 1934).

On Frugal Living:

"It is not the man who has too little, but the man
who covets more, that is poor."
-- Seneca, the Younger
Roman Philosopher ca 4BC-65AD

[1]

Introduction & How To Read This Book

People began outfitting vehicles for camping only a few decades after the automobile was first developed. It was an extension of horseback or wagon travel. The traveler would just stop alongside the road and camp for the night; first with bedrolls, later in tents. With the growth of the automobile, motorcars and trailers were converted for overnight use on the roadside.

As roads and highways improved, people started traveling further. Sometimes the travel was to reach

1

a destination, sometimes it was just for the sake of traveling. Travel was no longer an undertaking of necessity; it became a recreational pursuit. As trailers and converted motorcars became more defined, they picked up a new name: recreational vehicle. During the 1960s, a marketing term for these conversions was devised: RV.

Today, many people have discovered the joy of traveling with their families on weekends and vacations in an RV. It is an inexpensive way to travel to various cities and states across the USA. Families find that this mode of travel introduces children to sightseeing, museums, and historical sites. Families can camp, fish, swim, boat, and participate in other activities to help their children know and appreciate nature and the great outdoors. Hiking and spending time with the children teaches family values. Living together in nature and working side-by-side doing campsite chores can be accomplished without the pull of television, video games, and the other toys that remain behind at home.

Some folks do not start to explore the United States in an RV until after their children are grown and/or they have retired.

There is a whole industry catering to these RVers, providing them with products and services designed to make their camping experience better, more comfortable, and even adding some of the technology and toys from home.

Most RVers start by upgrading from tent camping to anything that gets them off the ground. They may graduate in stages, first to a tent trailer, then to a travel trailer, a 5th wheel, or even a motorhome, depending upon their financial means and personal preferences. Some families begin at the 5th wheel trailer or Class A motorhome level. Some graduate to monstrous motor buses with all of the latest conveniences: a clothes washer and dryer, dishwasher, ice machine, and built-in central vacuum.

These decisions usually depend on the life that they are accustomed to and how they want to travel. For many, their use is mostly personal and occasionally.

This level of use seldom offers any tax deductions except those related to having a second home: deducting only the mortgage interest and sometimes the vehicle tags.

Then there are the part-time RVers. These individuals live part of the year in a "brick and stick" home they own, but travel extensively for three to six months at a time often in another state or states. Other RVers have no permanent home but live full-time in their RV. They migrate with the sun. The summer months find them in the north and they drive south in the winter.

Part-timers or full-timers may work temporary or seasonal jobs at a campground in a state park or national forest. Some follow construction sites or engineering projects as their employer moves around the country. They may be retired or semi-retired. Others travel to visit grandkids or to sightsee and offset their expenses by working seasonally while on the way. For some, working is the main purpose of the trip; sightseeing and visiting family is secondary.

How to Use This Book

The purpose of this book is not to make tax experts of you, but to help you understand the tax issues that you will face as you venture into the RV "lifestyle." It is not intended to be read from beginning to end like a novel but used as a reference book. After reading Chapter 1, review the remaining chapters and study those that apply to you and your particular situation. You are encouraged to read them all, of course, but the book is divided into sections for different types of RVers: the weekend and vacationer, the part-time traveler, and the full-timer.

Some of the material in each chapter may be duplicated because the book is designed for each RVer to get all the information they need by reading only those portions applicable to their own situation. If you should happen to read the same material in a couple of different chapters, that is okay. Reading all the chapters will re-enforce what applies to you while offering additional information you may use later if you decide to change your way of travel or your lifestyle. This book is made to serve you, even if the way you RV changes!

This book is written to help you save money on your taxes. Some of the costs of your RV and travel expenses may be a tax deduction, depending on whether they meet the right criteria. The chapters that follow will help the RVer who wants to lower his tax liability and is willing to structure his life to do so. It will also help every RVer understand when the tax savings may not justify the effort of recording and tracking all of the deductions.

Many times, I have been asked, "Can I write off my RV?" "The salesman at the RV dealership said that I could, is that true?" Well... maybe. I have heard many tax accountants and tax preparers say, "No, you can't deduct any of it! Remember, it's a <u>recreational</u> vehicle." Alternatively, "If you don't have a home base, then you cannot deduct any of the RV, except the tags and interest." There is a lot of confusion about what can and what cannot be deducted when you purchase an RV. Your deductions (or lack thereof) depend on how you plan to use it.

People who work as they travel around the country in their RVs, develop a more complex, involved tax return to retain all their deductions. Working in various states necessitates filing a state return in each state where they work. The correct preparation of a multi-state return can be very complicated. Of all the 50 states, 41 use an income tax system for their major state revenue and there are 41 different methods to calculate the tax ... each with different rules and procedures.

I lived this lifestyle for almost 17 years. My wife and I lived in a motorhome, worked seasonally, and conducted a business while we traveled. I want to share my experiences both as an RVer who worked while traveling on the road and as a tax preparer with my own tax practice, a business that catered to preparing income tax returns for other RVers who worked as they traveled.

2]

What Is My Background?

Education

When I was discharged from the U.S. Army, I attended the University of Texas at El Paso. I graduated with a Bachelor of Arts in Business Administration. I spent the next couple of years in Oklahoma City selling radio and newspaper advertising as well as insurance. For five years after that, I was a state field auditor collecting state unemployment tax returns and performing claimant investigations for the Oklahoma Employment Security Commission. During that time, I began and completed evening courses toward a graduate degree at the University of Central Oklahoma. In 1978, I was awarded a Masters Degree in Business Administration. With my brand new degree in hand, I started a consulting business dedicated to helping entrepreneurs and small business owners learn how to keep their records on a manual bookkeeping system. This was 2-3 years before the personal computer was developed and 10 years before QuickBooks and other similar accounting software packages were available, so the owner-maintained computerized bookkeeping systems we have today did not exist.

As their businesses flourished and their accounting needs grew, I provided a bookkeeping staff to maintain records for them. I would show them how to analyze their financial statements and how to use them for management purposes. I taught them how to prepare a budget and to scratch out a simplified break-even point on the back of a napkin. I wanted them to know how financial statements could (and should) be used for management purposes, not just for tax preparation.

Not long after I started my practice, I realized that if I wanted to prepare income taxes for individuals and for the various business entities that they were forming (including corporations and partnerships) I needed to expand my knowledge even further, so I began to study for the Enrolled Agent exam given by the IRS.

What Is An Enrolled Agent?

After the Civil War, the U.S. Government needed staff to help the general public organize their records and present their claims for crops and livestock lost during the war. In 1884, the government empowered a body of men to work with the public and authorized them to prepare the necessary forms for filing claims for restoration. These men were given the title of Enrolled Agents and were issued "Treasury Cards" as a means of identification to show the public that they had the power of advocacy to represent them. The use of these Enrolled Agents diminished during the last years of the 19th century as the restoration cases were finally completed and the paperwork made its way through the U.S. Treasury Department and the courts.

In 1913, our current income tax system was devised. It consisted of only four pages, one of which was instructions. It is unfortunate that we do not have that simplicity today! The newly established Internal Revenue Service decided to call upon the Enrolled Agents still registered, to help teach the public how to fill out their new tax returns and submit them with appropriate payments.

Today the Enrolled Agent designation, E.A., is awarded to individuals who successfully pass a two-day test covering corporate, partnership, and individual income taxes. It also covers gift tax, estate tax, payroll tax, and all versions and levels of taxes that are administered by the Federal Government. You may find more information about the designation on the Internal Revenue Service's website, www.irs.gov/taxprofessionals/enrolled-agents.

I had decided that I did not want to perform financial audits or to work with publicly held corporations, so

I did not want to become a Certified Public Accountant. My clientele consists of individual business owners, small closely-held corporations, and partnerships. I wanted my focus to be on managerial and tax accounting not financial accounting and auditing. Interestingly, many of my friends who did sit for and pass the CPA exam decided afterwards that did not want to perform certified financial audits either, Their practices were much like mine.

I had been in practice for six years when I was awarded my Enrolled Agent Certificate in April 1984.

My Practice

For nearly 20 years I served the general public in Oklahoma City, performing monthly, quarterly, and annual bookkeeping services. My firm prepared payroll checks, quarterly payroll reports, and monthly sales tax reports. Once my staff completed the monthly accounting, they brought me the financial statements. I would examine for accuracy and thoroughness and meet with the client on a monthly or quarterly basis. We would review the statements, analyze the figures, and discuss their meaning. We compared the monthly or quarterly results with their budget and used that data to plan steps to be taken during the coming months to improve their business.

During this time, I was deeply involved with my three children's lives. It seemed to be a whirlwind of scouting, band practice, orthodontic appointments, and Friday night ball games. I was also involved in the OKC Chamber of Commerce, church activities, my professional public accounting societies, a couple of breakfast associations, and a local club for British sports cars. I had a vintage 1973 Triumph Spitfire at that time and was very active with the local Triumph auto club and the Sports Car Club of America. I had several clients who raced sports cars as a sideline business. We struggled with the IRS to prove that their racing was a legitimate business activity and not just a hobby.

My daily routine often started at 6 a.m. with a business breakfast meeting and often ended late in the evenings. Occasionally, during "tax season" or some deadline period, I worked until after midnight.

In the spring of 1993, my wife of 25 years surprised me by asking for a divorce. After the property division and settlement, I began to pick up the pieces and re-organize my life. I was feeling stressed and tired most of the time. I missed a few deadlines and began to feel I was no longer offering clients my best service. Being a workaholic had left me burned out.

My kids were all out of the house and mostly on their own. The youngest was finishing her senior year at the University of Oklahoma and living in her sorority house. I was ready for a break and a complete change in scenery. The 2-3 week tours that I took annually with my Triumph club were not enough time away anymore. It was not enough to refresh me for another year. I felt that there must be more to life. I began to re-examine my own goals and the dreams I had allowed to languish.

A Life Changing Event

On April 19, 1995, the Murrah Federal office building in downtown Oklahoma City was bombed. It was blown up by a terrorist at 9:02 on a Tuesday morning. A lady that I'd been dating, Charisse, worked in the Federal Reserve Bank building, only a block away from the Murrah Federal building. I had heard nothing from her and she was not answering her phone. I did not know until mid-afternoon whether it was her building that had been bombed. My business partner's wife was in the Murrah Federal building. He heard nothing about her until late that evening. She was severely injured, but was alive.

That day had a great and immediate impact on Charisse and me. We begin to feel that this life was too short; that our lives could be dramatically and suddenly altered or ended by situations beyond our control. We decided to take steps do the things that we really wanted to do with our lives now and quit waiting.

I had been talking to an accountant friend about merging our practices. He wanted us to purchase a large office building, utilize part of it for our new-to-be formed joint practice, and lease out the remainder. We had already been looking at several potential buildings. Although I had been enthusiastic a few months earlier, things had changed for me. I told him, "I have a better idea, why don't you buy my practice? I'll head for Costa Rica, Key West, Cape Cod, or someplace ... I just want to get the hell out of Dodge!"

That was in April. By May, we had worked out a plan and in June I had a contract for him to purchase my practice. It was not the best timing for me retirement-wise, since I was carrying a fair amount of debt at that time. Nevertheless, I was free! I could leave and feel assured that my clientele were in good hands and their accounting needs would be well-served.

I had been dreaming, reading books about men who built or bought cruising sailboats and sailed around the world. I was inspired and began to look at boats. My wise new wife, Charisse, pointed out that these sailors lived on the coast, had always lived near the water, and considered sailing second nature. The learning curve for this endeavor was going to be extraordinarily steep for me, a landlubber from Oklahoma who had never been on a body of water too large for me to swim across. She said if that was what I really wanted, she was willing and we could see how we liked it. Of course, she was right. I subsequently began, instead, to investigate how a landlubber could go cruising on land.

Introduction to RVing

A friend gave me a book written by a couple who did just what I wanted to do. *Full-Time RVing: Life On The Open Road* by Bill Moeller and Jan Moeller, Trailer Life Publications, 1995; tells of their experience in RVing. They bought a 5th wheel trailer and toured the continental United States. My interest was piqued. After searching, I found a book by another couple doing almost the same thing. An *Alter-*

native Live Style: Living and Traveling Full-Time In A Recreational Vehicle by Ron and Barb Hofmiester, R&B Publications, 1993, tells of their travels as they drove a motorhome and towed a small car behind it.

I began to make a plan. I looked at various motorhomes and we planned to set sail... on land. I would tow a car rather than a dingy. By June of that year, we bought a 30' motorhome, sold most of our possessions and stored some things (including Charisse's grandmother's china, and some treasured trophies) in a public storage unit.

In September, we hit the road for the first time on our new adventure. My sister and brother-in-law were supportive and gave us an Escapees RV Club membership for a wedding present. We were heading for New England with planned stop at an Escapees Escapade convention in Ohio on the way.

Our intent was to travel and see all that we could of this country for a couple of years; then return to Oklahoma to re-start our lives in another home with new jobs or businesses.

We spent 6 weeks in New England; trying to eat all of the lobster that had been caught on the coast that season. We visited every museum that we could find. It was a wonderful, relaxing trip. We visited all the different places we had seen in movies, read about in novels, in the news, or in history books.

The trip brought our big country to life and brought a greater depth of understanding of just what it means to be an American; to walk the hallways and climb the same stairs that Andrew Jackson, the Founding Fathers, and Elvis Presley had walked. (Not all in the same building, of course.) We gained an appreciation of the countryside and enjoyed the views that inspired writers such as Nathaniel Hawthorn and Washington Irving.

I grew up in Oklahoma and had spent most of my life there. Most of the buildings I knew were no more than 50-75 years old. In the cities we toured in the East, we saw houses and buildings 200 years old and occasionally 300 years old.

The Decision to Go Fulltime

We returned to Oklahoma City after that first fall trip. I had promised the accountant who had taken over my tax practice that I would come back to work and help with the transition during the first tax season.

We were so full of excitement. It had been a 3-month long camping weekend, in which we did not have to return to work each Monday. We stopped in beautiful campgrounds on the edge of lakes, toured Graceland, visited the Hermitage, and thoroughly enjoyed the delicious treats and interesting sites of Amish country.

I had toured the East before, while driving a British sports car alone and while caravanning with other Triumph enthusiasts. I had flown to other parts of the country on business trips. I stayed in hotels, sleeping in strange beds and living out of a suitcase.

This trip was different. I was with my wife in a 30' motorhome. We slept in our own bed every night. We had all our clothes in our closet and chest. We did not have to pack and repack each day.

We had our own food and cooked our own meals in our own kitchen. I had my library of books to read and home movies to watch. I even had my guitar to serenade my wife at night while sipping a scotch or brandy from my favorite glass sitting around an open campfire.

We had our home with us. We towed a Mazda to drive for our sightseeing. We were traveling and sightseeing, doing exciting new things every day …while still living at home. What's not to like about that?

We re-thought our original plan of doing this for just a year or two. If we could find some way to earn money while we traveled, we could live like this! Wow.

We worked through the winter of 1995 and the spring of 1996 and began to plan where we could go next, while still working seasonally, doing tax preparation.

Working On the Road

After tax season in the spring of 1996, we left to explore South Texas. We visited Houston, Galveston, and Corpus Christi to make employment contacts for the following year. I did not yet know about Workamper® News and the job opportunities listed there. That would have made the search so much easier!

We stopped in Livingston, Texas at the Escapees RV Club national headquarters. We already received the club's magazine each month and had stayed at several of their campgrounds. We were so impressed with them that we changed the wedding present of an annual membership to a lifetime membership and became Texas residents.

After a month of handing out resumes in tax offices and meeting tax accountants in cities along the Texas coast, we turned back north and headed for a cooler climate. It was late June and was getting hot, so we hurried up to the northern states and spent the rest of the summer traveling the Dakotas, Montana, Washington, and Oregon. We spent a leisurely fall along the western states, before heading south to Corpus Christi for the winter.

Corpus Christi Tax Office

We did not arrive until late December. That, coupled with the fact that I had not started searching for a position early enough in the year, meant most of the "plum" tax preparations jobs were already filled.

That year, I worked for a national tax preparation chain. I reasoned that this would be a good experience; one that could result in a position I could take with me to any city in the country. The reality was that the pay was minimal, especially for my experi-

ence and background. The chain's office was designed for walk-in customers only and the traffic
was rather light.

Map Advertising Sales

During that tax season, I discovered Workamper®
News, and found a position with a campground site
map company selling ads to local businesses. We
were given campsites with hookups to use for 2-3
weeks while selling advertising to local businesses
to be printed on the campground's site map. This
could be done while we traveled across the country
from RV park to RV park.

After tax season, we left Corpus Christi and began a
tour with Southeast Publications selling advertising
to businesses surrounding RV parks across the na-
tion. For my efforts we received a free campsite
with utilities and a percentage of the sales (after
printing and production costs). We went to Las Vegas, Southern California, back to Arizona, Oklaho-

ma, Alabama, Virginia, Pennsylvania, and finally Skowhegan, Maine. We finished up with a final sales job back at an RV park in Fort Worth, Texas.

I enjoyed the work. I have always enjoyed sales work. We saw even more of the U.S.A. than the year before, but barely made enough to cover our travel expenses. Since I still had a significant amount of business debt, I needed to earn more money.

I talked with other sales representatives and discovered that some of them made good money, but it had taken them several years to get to that point. They were traveling all of the time and had a set route they traveled. A few were making six-figure incomes, but they led harried lives hustling from one job to another, sometimes working two parks at once. I had escaped from that kind of workaholic stress when I sold my Oklahoma City practice. I didn't want it back. I had made big changes to live a more relaxed, enjoyable life.

Houston Tax Accounting Office

In late November, we arrived in Huston, Texas and I found a position with an accounting firm in the west edge of the city. I worked there for about two years, still living in the motorhome taking short trips on weekends and holidays.

When we traveled, we liked to visit the Northwestern states of Washington, Oregon, and Montana but it was a long drive to get there from Southeast Texas. We felt that it was time to move on. We wanted to relocate to Arizona for work during tax seasons. That move would cut a thousand miles off the trip to our favorite areas.

Arizona Tax Office

In September, I found a seasonal tax preparation position with a large firm in Tempe, AZ for the following spring. It paid well and we made plans to come back in January of the following year before heading to Death Valley, CA for their annual 49ers Celebration. We were in the Phoenix Valley for almost 3 years, working during tax seasons and traveling the rest of the year.

During the third year, I posted signs around Phoenix Valley for bookkeeping and tax work. We did not leave that summer. We stayed and worked all year. We were in Arizona long enough that a state police officer, who had seen me frequently, inquired about my residency. He insisted that I obtain an Arizona auto licenses plate and I was fined $86 for late registration. When I applied for an Arizona license plate, the tag agent said that in order to apply for a state tag on the car, I would have to show proof of an Arizona auto insurance policy. When I asked my insurance company for Arizona insurance for the car, I was told I would need an Arizona driver's licenses. After I got the Arizona driver's license, everybody was happy.

When my wife needed surgery that fall, the question of our residency became an issue for our Texas-issued health insurance. I apparently shot myself in the foot with a driver's licenses in one state while claiming residency in another. Thankfully, Blue Cross/Blue Shield accepted our insurance claim as Texas residents, but that hassle was enough. We decided to move back to Texas and get ready to travel again. We would be traveling full-time and planned to work till we were out of debt and could support ourselves while on the road.

Kerrville Tax Office

In the fall of 2002, we relocated to Kerrville, Texas where I took over the tax/bookkeeping practice of a local CPA who had been asked to become the chief financial for the Kerrville Independent School District.

We thought about building or buying a house, but could not decide: In town or outside of town? Remodel an old house or build a new straw bale house? We knew that once our time was up in Kerrville, we would travel again, so we decided to buy a bigger motorhome.

We purchased a Pace Arrow, 35' wide body. It had a queen island bed, 6' of closet space across the back, a separate office/work area for me, and a bathtub big enough for Charisse to stretch out in. We had a small mansion on wheels.

We were in Kerrville for 6 years. I became engrossed with the local Chamber of Commerce and other organizations that enmeshed our lives just as they had in Oklahoma, but this time was different. We knew what we were doing and made plans to leave again from the day we arrived. We planned to get out of debt and give away all of our storage stuff except grandmother's china.

On The Road Again

When our time was up in 2008, I sold that bookkeeping / tax practice to a local accounting firm and we hit the road again. This time I kept a small clientele of tax clients that were scattered around the country. Some were in Oklahoma, some in Houston, some in Arizona. These clients were not part of the Kerrville practice and not part of the sale. Now, I had enough clients to support us and I could serve them via the Internet, no matter where we traveled. Wheeee!!

After being on the road again for a year and a half, Charisse developed some health issues that made traveling in the motorhome uncomfortable for her. It became apparent that her health would not permit us to travel anymore. We decided that if it was not fun for her to travel, it was time for us to hang up the keys. At that point, we had been traveling for almost 17 years.

Those are years that we will never forget. Sometimes we feel that they were the best years of our lives, but who knows? Life goes on. Being traveler's means we can quickly adjust to any hand that we are dealt.

Today, we are enjoying our lives here in the little house we bought in Mesa, Arizona. I have another Triumph sports car, a TR6 this time, and we added a new member to our family: a rescued, 10 month old, Boston terrier puppy named Ben.

[3]

What Is Your Domicile?

State of Residency

Everyone has a domicile or a state of residence.
Generally, it is the state in which you reside. It is
the place you call "home." A state of residency is
declared when you register to vote or register a vehicle. When you take out a health or life insurance
policy or auto insurance, a state of residency is declared.

Health and life insurance policies are regulated by
each state. Each state has its own laws regarding
insurance including: types of insurance, the various
limits, deductibles, and other issues that pertain to

coverage and the responsibilities of the issuing company to the citizens of their state. Each state has a State Insurance Board to oversee the insurance companies wanting to sell insurance policies in their state. Each insurance company must be accepted by the state insurance board and must meet their requirements. Each health policy must be written for the residents of that particular state.

If a resident of State A were to take out a health policy that was written for State A, and then were to move to State B and establish a new residency, the insurance company could deny coverage for a medical claim simply because the policyholder was no longer a resident in the state where the policy was written. If the insurance company is notified beforehand that the policyholder is moving to another state and is changing their domicile, the company can usually re-issue the policy that meets the regulations for the new state.

The problem is when the insurance company is not informed about the move and change in residency.

They may not be licensed for your new state. Even though you have made timely monthly premiums, the company could (and probably would) deny coverage -- especially if they are presented with a large claim at the same time. They may be required to return your premiums, but you would still be without insurance coverage. Some of the large multi-state companies might convert the policy to your new state, but it's an iffy situation. If a claim is being considered, the outcome may be obvious.

The same principle holds true for automobile insurance. Each state also has different laws to regulate the issuance of driver's licenses and the registration of motor vehicles.

If you have a truck or automobile registered in Texas, and drive it to the state of California, the state of California cannot stop you simply because you do not have a California emissions sticker or a California safety inspection test. You have a Texas vehicle and you are Texas resident, regulated by Texas laws. But, if a California state trooper observes that you have been the area over 6 months and are working there as a potential "new resident," the trooper may try to enforce California laws, and require you to obtain a California drivers license and vehicle registration with the required emission and safety tests. So, if you are not a resident, you need to be able to prove that you are just traveling through or are working only temporarily.

The way you declare your domicile or state of residency may vary depending on your chosen state. Generally, it includes registering your vehicles, applying for driver's licenses, applying for insurance, either vehicle or health (or both), and registering to vote.

Other methods for establishing a domicile are library cards, local religious congregation or temple affiliation, or other fraternal memberships such as Elks lodge or Rotary Club. Some of these choices do not require that you be a "resident" but will allow "guest" members. All of these declarations combined are how you show your state residency.

Taxation

Your state residency determines in which state you will file your taxes as a resident and which you file as a non-resident. All of your taxable income is reported to your resident state and taxes are calculated according to their laws. If you have a pension that was earned in a different state than your current resident state it is only taxed in your current residential state. The state in which you worked and earned a pension, cannot tax you on that income if you are no longer a resident of that state. That has not always been the case.

Michigan and California are famous for aggressively pursuing former residents and taxing them on the withdrawal of pensions that had been earned in their state even though the retiree had moved and properly established a residence in a new state. A U.S. Supreme Court ruling, back during the 1980s settled that in favor of the taxpayers who had moved to a state that did not have a state income tax.

Presently, pensions and annuities are not taxed by the state in which the account is held and pays the funds but by the state which is your residence or domicile, according to Federal Public Law 104-95, enacted in 1996. Rental income, income from partnerships, and S corporation income are under different rules. They are usually taxed by the state in which the project is held, but that may differ with certain states. Self-employment income and wages are always held as taxable to the state in which they are earned.

If you have earned income in a non-residential state, that income is reported to the non-resident state and any taxes that will be due will be payable to the non-resident state. It is also reported as income to your residential state, any taxes due to your residential state would be calculated, a credit for the taxes paid on that out-of-state income to the non-residential state is allowed and is applied to the tax due to the residential state.

This procedure relieves you of double taxation unless the non-residential state charges a higher tax rate than your residential state. This technique of calculating income taxes was started back in the 1980's by the State of Kansas. It was a way for them to increase their revenue without raising their tax rates. It put the short-term earnings of non-resident taxpayer in a higher tax bracket. Kansas' method eventually spread to other states so that now it a common practice with many states.

If you have "significant" retirement or some other non-earned income, consider moving your domicile to one of the non-income tax states. However, it would be unwise to move to a state with no income tax, if you have to pay an extra $2,000 in property taxes and insurance just to save $200 in state income tax.

Add up your income and the costs and expenses for a given state and calculate what you will owe in state income taxes. You do not have to be precise, a good estimate will work. Then try that for a prospective state. The difference in tax due may be quite significant or it may be minimal, but you will have the calculations and actual numbers you need to make an informed decision.

Multiple "Domiciles"

Many RVers will establish a domicile in one of the states that does not have a state income tax (Florida, Texas, South Dakota, Wyoming, Nevada, Washington, Alaska, Tennessee and New Hampshire), usually to avoid having to pay income taxes on their retirement pensions. However, when they want to purchase another RV some will try different schemes to show that they are residents of a state that has no sales tax.

They will set up a mailing address in the no-sales-tax state and say that they are now residents of that state. Sometimes they will get by with this for a while, but they are usually caught within a couple of years. Not only is this unethical, it is considered illegal in some states and may subject the RVer to a hefty fine.

You are taking a huge chance if you select an eclectic mix of states claiming residence in one without income tax, another without sales tax, and a third for some other reason. If you happen to work in a non-residential state like California, California could claim that you have not declared any particular state as a domicile. They could then say the State of California has the right to tax all of your pension income as a resident of their state and they would most likely prevail in that claim. Whoops! That can cause a painfully large tax bill, especially painful if you are not prepared for it. If you try to claim various states as a resident at the same time, you will not have much of a defense against such charges.

Home Base In Different State Than Domicile

Some people have asked me about having a home base in a different state than their domicile state. Will it qualify as a residence to enable to deduct the away-from-home expense? Their thinking was to have a domicile in Texas or Florida or any one of the no income states. But, they are no longer or seldom in the area that they claim as their home. They have become RV full-timers.

They decide to purchase a new home where their friends are or where they customarily spend much of their time. They may even work in the area. They try to meet the minimal requirements for the address to qualify as a home base, but they will be violating one of the criterions necessary to be eligible for the deduction. (In Chapter 4 "What Expenses May I Deduct," I discuss the criteria needed to claim the away-from-home deductions.) They would have to move their domicile to the new state if they want that for a home base. It is an issue of confusing the declaration of your residential state. You might "get by with it" for a couple of years, until audited, but you should not count on it for a permanent solution.

If the new home is worthwhile, you should consider changing your state of residence. Talk with a tax professional and discuss how much your state income tax liability will be in the new state. It may not be as great as you fear. If you customarily claim the standard deduction, the income tax levied by the new state may be less than the tax savings of deducting your away-from-home expenses.

While none of us is particularly fond of having to pay income taxes, it is necessary to operate our government, build our roads and bridges, and support our military defense. Personally, I have less of a problem with paying taxes than I do with what the wasteful way our government handles the tax funds they receive. Maybe it is because I know and understand the tax laws and I know that I am paying the lowest amount of tax for the level of income that I earn, that payment of that tax is not so painful for me. I want to help you pay the lowest amount for your level of income and help to reduce the pain for you as well.

Renting Out The Home Base

Some workampers have asked me about renting out their home base. They want to keep a home base just to be able to deduct the away-from-home expenses while they are away working at a Workamper job. They also want to rent out the home base in order to help pay the mortgage and the costs of home ownership.

If they do rent out the home base, they no longer have a home: it has become a rental house. Rental income is reported on the Schedule E, page 1. All of the associated expenses: mortgage interest, real estate taxes, insurance, utilities, supplies, maintenance, etc., are deducted to arrive at the net rental income. The net rental income is then carried to Form 1040, page 1. What they have done is eliminate their away-from-home deductions, since they are no longer duplicating their home costs while working.

That may not be a bad deal. If they like the house and want to come back to it someday, renting may be a good way to defray costs, even if doing so eliminates their away-from-home deductions. Also, if the real estate market is down in the area, renting the home is a good way to help hold on to the house until it can be sold.

Home rental is not for the faint of heart. You are going to be an absentee landlord. You must be adamant in collecting the rent. If you let a tenant be late one month because "the baby was sick," you will have the same problem another month with "having to repair the car," then it will be "I lost my job, but I'll pay you double next month." You must be an astute judge of character to be able to accurately predict which perspective tenant will have a ethical compulsion to pay their rent on time and will properly care for your property.

Problems may be alleviated if you hire professional real estate property management to find tenants, collect rent, and keep the property maintained. The management fee will be somewhere in the 10% range of the rental income and they may charge additional for the maintenance.

When you return, you may find that a tenant has repainted the house, uprooted your favorite bush, or made some other unexpected changes to the house. If you have a slovenly tenant, you may find your house damaged from neglect or intentional destruction. Be prepared for that.

I do not want to discourage you from renting your house if you want to keep the house and reduce your cash outflow. If you have the personality for it, it is an excellent investment. Properly handled, rental property is one of the best investments, as well as one of the few remaining tax shelters. If conditions are right, buying, fixing up, and renting real estate it is one of my favorite investments.

[4]

What Expenses May I Take?

Allowable Deductions

The Internal Revenue Code allows us to deduct from
our income all expenses that are deemed "ordinary
and necessary" to the production of our income.
There are reams of pages that discuss just what is
meant by "ordinary and necessary." They are too
detailed and dependent on individual circumstances
to explain all the possible technical points here. Although I discuss those points in detail when counsel-
ing with each of my clients, for the purposes of this
book I will have to limit the scope to general expla-
nations and descriptions.

Job Search Expenses

Generally, these are costs and expenses incurred to search for and travel to your next work location. These expenses cannot be claimed when seeking a new career. Allowable expenses require that you search of a job in your current occupation. When defining your current or past work, use the broadest description of that line of work and the broadest description of the new job with the intent to keep the two job descriptions as similar as possible.

You can deduct travel expenses. You can elect to claim either the standard mileage deduction or the actual expenses, meals, and lodging required to get to the job or interviews.

All employment fees and expenses to access lists available jobs are also deductible. For example, specialized subscriptions such as Workamper® News, both their paper edition and the online version are deductible expenses. You may deduct any expenses for networking for a new job. If you pay for a Workamper® News's Gold Membership, for example, you may deduct that cost. If your employer pays for any of these expenses, you may only deduct them if employer includes the reimbursement as income on your W-2. If your employer reimburses you during a later year, you must include the reimbursement as income in the year in which it was received.

When you travel to an area to look for a new job or to work in your usual occupation, you may be able to deduct the travel expenses to and from the area. The amount of time you spend on personal activities compared to the amount of time you spend looking for work is an important factor in determining whether the trip is primarily to look for a new job or for personal reasons. Be sure to record this detail in a travel log book maintained for travel dates and purposes.

According to the Internal Revenue Code, you cannot deduct any of these job search expenses if there is a substantial break between the end of your last job and the time you begin looking for a new one.

However, the IRS does not address the definition of a "substantial break." Be it three weeks, three months or three years, the definition depends heavily on the length of time spent on your previous job, the type of job it was, and the efforts spent looking for the new one. You may apply a liberal interpretation, but it would be wise to keep this in mind. Sometimes the need for employment does not happen when someone starts to travel either part-time or on a full-time basis. If a sabbatical break is necessary for rest from stress, emotional trauma, or for some other reason, be sure to write that down in your travel log.

Other work-related or job search expenses such as postage, resumes, cost to have resumes written, or coaching for the preparation of the resume are deductable. Jaimie Hall Bruzenak's book, "*Support Your RV Lifestyle! An Insider's Guide to Working On The Road*" offers great advice to help you to write a resume targeted to employers looking for seasonal and recurring jobs. She also offers assistance with writing your resumes at:

http://www.rvlifestyleexperts.com/rv-books/resume-assistance/ Both of these would be deductible.

Away-From-Home Expenses

For those RVers who still have a home and only travel during the summer or during the winter, there are some special deductions allowed because your housing costs are duplicated when you are working away-from-home.

This means that the job search and the job take you away from a home that you've established but must leave while you are away working. This "home" or "home base" may be a house or condominium that you own or a house or apartment you rent. The expenses for the capital outlay or rent of the lodging, utilities, taxes, insurance, etc., have to be duplicated while you are away in order to qualify.

Everyone has a cost of living expenses for housing, utilities, etc. These are personal expenses and are not deductible. If, however, your work requires you to leave temporarily (defined as less than a year) you may deduct the duplicated costs.

In order for the away-from-home expenses to be deductible, you must meet three criteria:

1. You perform part of your work or business in or near the metropolitan area of your main home.
2. You have living expenses at your main home that must be duplicated because you are away-from-home.
3. You have not abandoned the area in which your claimed home is located.

This means: 1.) you must perform some of your work in the area that you are calling home, as well as in the away-from-home work area. Sometimes this is a difficult activity to accomplish or to prove. Where you perform your work is your "tax home". If you do none of your work in the area that you are calling a "home base" then you do not qualify for the away from home rules. 2.) If you are renting out your "home base" then you are not duplicating your living expenses. If you have merely purchased or rented a lot year around while you travel, it is questionable whether you have to duplicate anything while you are away. Much depends on the cost of the "home base", the improvements and the services maintained while you are away. 3.) If you abandon the area that you have called home and no longer return or seldom return there, you may need to choose a new domicile.

If you should meet all of these criteria, then your deductible expenses include: rent for lodging, i.e. motel, or (in the case of the RVer) the campsite rental fee, as well as utilities for electric and fees for hookups. You may also deduct food, either dining out and/or groceries and incidentals such as laundry, household supplies.

Sometimes a standard meal allowance may be deducted instead of actual expenses, but this is a complex area and must be evaluated on a case-by-case method. Bear in mind that the cost of food, whichever method used, may only be deducted for the working spouse. If both spouses are working, then the food costs for both may be deducted. The cost for housing (rent, lease, or campground fees) is not more or less just because there are two of you. In addition, travel to the job site is not any different unless one of you drives the personal car and follows the spouse driving the RV rig.

A mail-forwarding service only will not qualify as a "home base." Several RVers have tried this and have failed under an IRS audit. There is no structure to being duplicated while you are working away from home. A mail-forwarding address will, however, serve as your official mailing address for use on your driver's license, vehicle registration, voter registration, and the mailing of your tax returns.

The Itinerant Worker

Some RVers have sold their traditional home and travel constantly. These snowbirds may spend the winters in the warm southern states such as Florida, Texas, New Mexico, Arizona, or California. Then, in the spring, they begin to head north or to a higher altitude and a cooler temperature. They work at a temporary job while in the South during the winter and another job in the summer in the North. Sometimes they will work a short-term job in between.

Since they do not have a home base, they are never able to meet the away-from-home rules. These individuals are termed itinerant workers by the IRS. Their tax home is wherever their work is and they are never away-from-home because they take their home with them. Remember the bumper sticker: "Home is where I park it." Without a home base, they are not allowed to deduct any campground fees, utilities, or food costs while they are on a job. They may still deduct the travel expenses as they travel to new job assignments, but must keep an accurate log of their travels and keep separate the travel expenses of going to a job and traveling just to see family and friends. If they stop to see the Grand Canyon or some other site that is geographically on the way, that is okay, but they should make sure that sightseeing does not overshadow or dominate the purpose of the trip.

Deductibility Of An RV Site

If your employer furnishes you a campsite with hook-ups and requires you to stay on-site, then this is considered a job requirement or condition of employment and is not taxable income nor an expense even if you are eligible to deduct your away-from-home expenses. If you are paid in full for all of the hours that you work and then have to pay for your campsite, the cost of the campsite may be deducted if it is a job requirement that you stay at the campground.

Some RVers, such as those defined as itinerant workers, are not always eligible to deduct these items. Because of this, the IRS promotes employers to issue a W-2 or 1099 for this benefit. I feel this is done to encourage uninformed employers to report this as income even though it is a non-taxable benefit if it is for the convenience of the employer. Some ultra-conservative and uninformed tax preparers and bookkeepers will issue a W-2 or 1099 for their campground clients for this benefit even if it is not necessary.

When you are interviewing for a job, ask if you are required to live onsite and make sure the value of that site will not be included on your W-2 or 1099 since it is a job requirement for the benefit of the employer. If you are required to live on site, secure a signed statement to that effect. This statement should also indicate that it would not be included on your W-2 or 1099. Then pick up a campground brochure or download the campsite rates from the Internet and keep this information with your tax documents. If the value of the campsite is included in your income, you will then have the information to enable you to verify how much is included. If you cannot explain and dissuade the employer, then you may deduct the items on your Schedule A (if on a W-2), or on a Schedule C (if on a 1099) as a requirement of the job whether you are away-from-home or an itinerate worker.

Non-Deductible Expenses

There are some items that are not eligible for deduction, such as ordinary clothes that may be worn by the general public, even if it is called a "uniform." To be deductible as a uniform, the clothing must have the name of the employer printed, embroidered or otherwise permanently attached to it; a name tag that may be easily removed will not classify it as a uniform. Costumes, such as those for a docent at national or state park or a uniform at a theme park are also deductible.

The cost of a cell phone, fax machine, or Internet service are not be deducted unless solely for a job search; with no personal use. That would not be practical for your home phone or home Internet connection. If you have a business and these items are necessary for that business, they may be deducted. You must, however, have a second telephone line or cell number to be able to deduct a phone as a business expenses.

Full-time vs. Part-time RVers

You might think the full-time, itinerant worker is getting the short end of the deduction stick, but they do not have to duplicate their living costs. Living costs while out on the road, living in an RV, can be much less than having a large sum of money invested in a house. Just think about the capital invested, mortgage payments, real estate taxes, insurance, utilities, repairs and maintenance, and maintaining rent, utilities, and insurance on an apartment.

In the last chapter, I discussed having a "home base" in a state that is different from the domicile state. The domicile state in my example was chosen by an RVer merely because it did not have a state income tax. The individual seldom, if ever, visited that domicile state. That is fine for an itinerant traveler who always has his home with him, but if he tries to establish a home base in a different state, he is in danger of making an unintentional change in his domicile which could have unplanned negative tax consequences.

Occasionally, an itinerant worker may purchase a residence in a different state from their domicile of record in order to be closer to the area that they normally stay. They may purchase this home, sometimes meeting only the minimal requirements to be recognized as a home, with the sole intent to be eligible to claim the away-from-home expenses. They then fail to meet the third IRS criterion for this claim by abandoning the area where they claim their home is located.

Part of the time that Charisse and I were RVing, we had a home base and were able to deduct the away-from-home expenses, but most of the time we were considered full-timers. The itinerant periods of our lives were the periods of our lowest costs. When we had a home base, the costs that were being duplicated were always more than the deduction saved us in taxes.

If my wife and I were able to "hit the road" again, it would be as full-time, itinerant workers. There is so much freedom in not having to keep track of the costs of living. When we first paid off the mortgage on our house and the mortgage on the motorhome was so little that we did not qualify to claim itemized deductions. I no longer had to track all of our medical expenses, auto tags, charitable donations, and other tax expenses. We could donate to organizations or individuals without worrying about if our gift was "qualified." We gave from the heart, not for the tax deduction, and it made preparing our income taxes so much simpler.

[5]

Can I Deduct The RV?

One of the first things that RVers asks when they find out I prepare taxes is: "How can I deduct my RV?" or "The salesman said that I could write it all off the first year, is that true?" My first reaction is to ask if their barber thought that also; but, to be polite, I just ask how they plan to use the RV.

In order for RVs to be claimed as a second home, they must have the three essentials of 1) sleeping, 2) cooking and 3) toilet facilities. As a second home, they are then eligible to have the interest and taxes deducted on the Schedule A, the same as your stick and brick home.

Many RVers also want to find a way to deduct the initial cost, depreciation, and the maintenance of the RV. Whether or not that is possible depends how you plan to use it.

Construction Use

I have had clients, not necessarily RVers, who had construction businesses and traveled around the state doing remodeling jobs that would last for 2-3 weeks. Rather than spend money for a hotel, they bought a travel trailer, towed it to the job site and lived in it for the duration of the job. They would use it for a mobile office as well as living quarters while job lasted. They never used the trailer for any other purposes. For this taxpayer, the trailer is a 100% business asset and is fully depreciable and eligible for Section 179 expensing. If they were to use it for weekend trips with the family, we would have to pro-rate the cost of the trailer and claim only the percentage used for business.

Volunteering Pursuits

If an RV is used for touring and sightseeing during the summer by a couple who have a home base and volunteer their time at a national park in exchange for a campsite to lessen their costs, then there is no business use of the RV and no earnings motive. If they could document before the trip that their volunteered service is their main purpose of trip, they would have a different situation. Their fuel or mileage to the volunteer site will be deductible as a donation. If the RVer has a home base that he has to leave to volunteer his services, he could then be eligible for the away from home deductions. In order to take these deductions, arrangements must be made prior to the trip. The RVer should document contact with the national park or other non-profit organization for which they plan to volunteer before leaving. This will provide proof that the trip is primarily for the volunteer work, enabling the RVer to claim all eligible deductions.

Self-Employment Use

In another scenario, a part-timer RVer, having a home base in his state of domicile, might take their RV on the road (the only time it is used) to market and sell craft products that are produced at the home base. He takes them to fairs, craft shows, and has a schedule organized before he leaves home. His RV is only used to get to these craft shows. While he is away he is duplicating his living costs, so the use of the RV rig is 100% business use and would be fully depreciable.

Employee Use

If an RVer does not have a self-employed business, but only works at jobs RV parks or other businesses, then he does not have a business to charge it against. Any expenses that he might be eligible for are deducted a employee business expenses on Schedule A, subject to 2% of Adjusted Gross Income (AGI).

Percentage Of Use

In both of these cases, the cost of the RV may be deductible only if the RVer can prove, with a diary and an RV mileage log book, that this is the only use of the RV. The percentage of business use compared to the total use determines the percentage of the RV that may be depreciated or of the use that may be deducted.

The part-time RVers must watch their personal use and use the RV to seek work in their usual occupation. Any personal use may need to be calculated to reduce the business portion of the asset. They must show in their diary or RV logbook that the main purpose for a trip is to seek work or outlets to sell their crafts. Demonstrating that the jobs or suitable outlets for their products are not near their home would be helpful, if not essential.

Itinerant Full-Timer

For the itinerant full-timer, it is a different matter. Since he has no home base, and is constantly "at home" wherever he is, none of the lodging portion of the RV may be written off. Most RVs are not large enough to have a separate office space that is used exclusively for business for the self-employed and is unnecessary for the employed workamper.

I have seen one of the larger 5th wheels that had a separate, inside room at the back, able to be closed off from the rest of the RV. It was intended for a teenager traveling with parents and could be closed for them to have their own private area. I remember when I first saw this trailer, I thought about what a terrific tax office it would make. Someone who ran a virtual Internet office could have a nice workspace in that 5th wheel. Then that portion, maybe 20-25% of the 5th wheel could be deducted as business use.

The itinerant worker may deduct, as a job search expense, the travel from one job site to another, but must take care that he is searching for jobs in his usual line of work. He may deduct his mileage or his actual expenses getting to the job site. Actual expenses as defined by the IRS include: fuel, oil, tires, batteries, insurance, maintenance and depreciation; pro-rated by the business use percentage as shown by the mileage log.

Since the travel distance can be minimal many times for the full-timer, the standard mileage deduction may be greater and a lot simpler. Because of the high fuel usage of most RVs, if the RV rig is re-fueled each time before a business trip (do not we always) and the fuel receipts are kept with the mileage log, you could make a case that the cost of the fuel is the total cost of the trip. This would be a simplified, easy-to-keep method, though not necessarily the greatest write off.

Some of the newer RVs, called "toy haulers," have a separate compartment accessible from the back, for weekend enthusiast to take their 4-wheel ATVs or for auto racers to take a racecar. I have a client who set up an RV maintenance shop in this part of his RV, complete with a lathe, drill press, and other specialized equipment. He has taken Terry Cooper's The RV Professor's classes to become certified as an

RV maintenance technician (sometimes a tax deductible expense).

As a full-timer with no home base, he travels from campground to campground with no designated route and only goes where he wants for his personal pleasure. He has no designated route and only goes where he wants for his personal pleasure. He can deduct but little of his travel expenses, only the truck to go pickup parts and supplies, to a customer's site, to go to seminars, etc. There is some business use for travel for a specific job, but little. However, one-fourth of the 5th wheel is a RV maintenance workshop and will always be depreciable under the office in the home rules.

There are new simplified rules for claiming the office in the home deduction that have just been issued by the IRS. Announced on January 15, 2013 (Revenue Procedure 2013-13), it is effective for taxable years beginning after January 1, 2013. It allows the owner of a home-based business to deduct up to 300 sq ft at $5 per sq ft. There is a cap at a maximum of $1,500 per year. More information about this new rule may be found on the IRS website at: www.irs.gov/Newsroom/Simplified-Option-for-Claiming-Home-Office-Deduction-Starting-This-Year.

This is a greatly simplified method compared to the pro-ration of house basis, utilities, taxes, insurance, and maintenance that is required by the old method. The taxes and mortgage interest may still be deducted in full (not pro-rated) on the Schedule A. Since few of our RV toy haulers have that large of an area, this might make an easy deduction if you qualify.

The old method is still available for those who have a larger office in their home base that would qualify for the full larger deduction, but for small businesses this greatly simplifies things.

For the RVer, even a 12-foot compartment in an 8 foot wide body only comes to a 96 sq ft area and at $5 per sq ft a deduction of $480. It's not a biggie, but still an easy-to-calculate write-off. The home office, should you be eligible for it, is still limited to regularly and exclusive use for the business. This is mainly for the self-employed person; it would be hard to imagine a situation where a Workamper employer would require the use of the employee's home.

[6]

Are You An Employee Or Contractor?

Whether you are paid as an employee or an independent contractor makes a great difference in how and where you report your income. Most individuals work as an employee. They labor or provide personal services under an agreement, written or not, for an employer who has the authority to dictate the hours, place, and method of the engagement. They are paid hourly, weekly, monthly or by a percentage (commissions) or piecemeal (per item produced.)

The terms "independent contractor" and "contractor" are often interchangeable. A contractor is nearly always independent. Sometimes an employee may have a "contract" for the work he is to provide, what is expected of him, what vacations or holidays he is eligible for, etc. Technically, he is a contracted employee.

For our purposes here, I will use the term "contractor" as an independent contractor. He is self-employed, works for himself, and sets his own hours. He may work at the employer's premises or he may take the project home and work on it at his own shop. He usually has a substantial investment in tools and equipment. He sometimes works by the hour; sometimes by the project. He will bid on a project or will set his customary fee or hourly rate. He will generally prepare and issue an invoice for his work and present it to the employer for payment. Most of these points will occur with a contractor but not all of them are necessary.

Most importantly for a contractor, is that the employing agent does not withhold any FICA or Social Security taxes nor does he pay half of it to the Social Security Administration on behalf of the contractor. The contractor is responsible for the full payment of these taxes, but only on the net income after he has deducted all of his entitled expenses. His expenses are not reduced by 2% of AGI.

Does your employer withhold FICA and Medicare taxes? If so, then you are deemed an employee. Your expenses, should you be entitled to deduct any, are listed as employee business expenses on Schedule A, and subject to 2% of your Adjusted Gross Income (AGI).

You usually do not have a choice on whether you are considered an employee or a contractor. Per IRS regulations, if the employer exercises direct control over your duties, as to your hours, when to show up for work, how to do your work and the steps for your duties; and you do not have a significant investment in tools or equipment to do the job, then you are an employee.

This is a much-debated area between employers, tax accountants, and the IRS website (http://www.irs.gov) has a list of 20 criteria to determine whether a worker is an employee or an independent contractor.

Some employers will try to slant their agreement toward making the worker a contractor. This is easier for the small employer that has few or no other staff. In claiming incorrectly that the worker is a contractor, he does not have to track, calculate and file the quarterly payroll reports and does not have to pay half of the Social Security Tax. He simply issues a 1099-Misc for Non-Employee Compensation. A problem may arise, after filing the required 1099-Misc at the end of the year, if the Internal Revenue Service should audit the employer. If the IRS deems that the worker should have been an employee, the employer's records may be corrected to reflect the workers in question were employees. This adjustment may affect the worker's personal return, even after they already filed their taxes.

If you think that you are working in an employee position, verify that your employer is withholding the proper income, Social Security, and Medicare taxes. If he is not, he may intend to report you as a contractor and issue an earnings statement at the end of the year on a 1099-Misc.

When you have your return prepared, you may find that you are now responsible for paying both halves of your Social Security/Medicare tax as self-employment tax with your tax return since the employer did not withhold half of the tax from you and pay the other half yourself. Itemized deductions, personal exemptions, or any other tax losses will not offset this tax liability. That is not a pretty sight, especially when you are not expecting it. I have many low-income, self-employed clients that pay much more in self-employment tax than they pay in income tax. That is just the nature of self-employed work.

[7]

Can I Volunteer?

The majority of RVers that work while they travel, work at for-profit businesses. There are some RVers though, who work at jobs at national or state parks, volunteering their time and services checking in visitors, cleaning and maintenance of the campgrounds, etc. Others volunteer to build houses for Habitat for Humanity or help with emergency rescue for the Red Cross. If the organization is a qualified nonprofit organization, then the travel expenses to get there may be deducted as charitable donations rather than as employee business expenses. If you are required to camp on site but are not compensated with a free campsite, but must pay for it, that expense may be deducted as well if you are eligible for the away-from-home deductions. For an extra benefit, this donation deduction is not limited by 2% of your AGI. If it is not a qualified nonprofit entity though, you are not entitled to a charitable deduction.

If you volunteer for an organization, find out whether it is a qualified, 501(c)3, nonprofit entity before you reach an agreement to work for them if you are expecting to deduct your expenses. Volunteering for a qualified charitable organization must be the primary purpose of the trip, not just a second thought after you are already on your way to a personal vacation. If you have a home base and must pay for your own campsite and utilities while you are volunteering, then you may deduct these expenses as away-from-home costs also as charitable donations.

If it is a profit-oriented business that you will be volunteering for, it should be able to compensate you in addition to your campsite for your services.

If not, and you still feel that the arrangement is worthwhile because of the scenery, the amenities, etc; then continue on. Just remember that at the end of the year you do not get a deduction for any of your travel expenses since your efforts were not income or profit-motivated. The value of the campsite and hookups should still not be income to you if it is considered a working condition benefit. If you are an itinerant RVer and volunteer, the only amount that you may deduct are your expenses for transportation to get there, camping fees, utilities and meals en route.

You may not deduct anything for your time or labor unless it is reported as income to start with. If :

1. You were paid for your services as an employee or contractor,
2. Then endorsed your paycheck over to the nonprofit organization,
3. Then they issued you a W-2 or a 1099 at the end of the year,

Then you deduct the amount of your paychecks. You would have to count the total earnings but could only deduct the net payroll. This does not make economic sense to me. You may not have enough itemized deductions that would be greater than the standard deduction.

[8]

Which Business Entity?

If you are self-employed or an independent contractor, you must decide what type of entity your business will be. It could be a sole-proprietorship, a partnership, a limited liability company, or a corporation. How to choose the best business organization for your situation is fairly complex and beyond the scope of this book. However, you need to know the basics of how and where the results (income less expenses) are reported on your return.

Sole-Proprietorship

A sole-proprietorship is the easiest to establish and is the default status if no other choice is made.

The income and all necessary and ordinary expenses are reported on a Schedule C, which is part of your 1040. Your expenses will include the depreciation of any equipment and your auto expenses.

The net result or profit is subject to a calculation of your Social Security Tax, called Self-Employment tax. You have to pay both halves of the tax. (As an employee, your employer pays half the tax for you.) You do get to deduct half of the Self-Employment tax on the front page of the return. There are several other benefits the self-employed taxpayer is entitled to, but that, also is beyond the scope of this book.

Partnership

A partnership may be formed when two people launch and operate the same business. This could be a husband and wife team or two separate individuals. The income is accumulated by the partnership as are the expenses, then the net profit is then reported, to each, as income according to the percentage of ownership designated by the partnership agreement. This income is generally considered self-employment income and is subject to the self-employment tax just as in a sole-proprietorship. This partnership income is reported to each partner on a Form K-1, which is reported on each partner's Schedule E on their 1040.

Corporation

A corporation may be formed to operate a business. An attorney, licensed to operate in the state you choose for your domicile, should be engaged to form the corporation. The business will be registered in your domicile state as a corporate entity under the regulations of the state corporation commission. If formed in another state, then the corporation must also register as a foreign corporation in the state where it will be doing business.

A corporation must issue a W-2 to the shareholders/officers/employees. Quarterly or annual payroll reports will be required and the corporation will make payments for the income and Social Security taxes that are withheld. The corporation must file a separate income tax return (Form 1120) at the end of its fiscal year and the corporation pays its own income tax. The shareholders of the corporation declare dividends to be distributed to the shareholders proportionately to their owner- ship of the outstanding shares of stock.

These declared dividends are not considered as a deduction for calculating the corporate income tax. Each shareholder must report the dividends as income. Thus you can see, for small corpora- tions, where most of the income is distributed to the few (or only one) shareholders, the income is taxed twice.

S Corporation

To offset this double taxation, a corporation may file an election not to have its income taxable at the corporate level. This election is to make the corporation a Sub-Chapter S Corporation (Chapter S of the Internal Revenue Code). Net income un- der this business structure is reported on a Form

K-1 much like the partnership, but this income is not subject to the Self-Employment tax because the earned income of the shareholder/employee is reported on a W-2 as it is for a regular corporation.

Some taxpayers will try to beat the Social Security Tax by living on distributions and not paying themselves a salary from their S corporation. When the IRS finds this situation, it is a huge audit target. If the shareholder/officer is engaged in the daily operations of the company, they will reclassify all withdrawals and payments to the shareholder/officer as wages and prepare late filed quarterly tax reports with tax, penalties, and interest. A shareholder/officer should always show a reasonable salary paid to himself.

Limited Liability Company

A business entity may be formed as a Limited Liability Company (LLC). This structure offers restricted exposure to lawsuits and offers security for the personal assets of the organizing members.

If the LLC only has only one member, it is a Single Member Limited Liability Company (SMLLC). It may file as a sole-proprietorship. A SMLLC creates a business entity that will not have to have a second tax filing return, but will still get a limited liability status.

When an LLC applies for a Federal Employer Identification Number (EIN) with the IRS, a business structure and method of being taxed must be chosen: a partnership, corporation, or as an S corporation.

[9]

What Records Do I Keep?

Administrative Law

In the criminal U.S Court System, the accused is always considered innocent until the government proves him guilty, unlike the British counterpart where the accused, once investigated and charged, is considered guilty until the accused proves himself innocent. Their rationale is, that investigative research is made by the accusing authority and a determination is made as to guilt before any charges are brought; a reverse from our own system. The U.S. Court System, regarding administrative law, however, follows the British method of not bringing charges until all facts and evidence are examined. Once an IRS auditor examines the records and bank accounts, a meeting is held with their superior. The evidence is analyzed and charges are then made. A revised tax return is prepared and presented to the taxpayer for payment. It is up to the accused to prove their return with receipts and documentation of their claimed expenses.

Hence, it is the responsibility of the taxpayer to keep detailed, documented records to prove the income and expenses deducted on his tax return. If clear and accurate records are not kept, the IRS has auditing techniques to prove income that you received. They leave it up to you to prove deductions that you want to claim.

Paper or Digital?

A record keeping system, either a hard copy on paper or a digital file on a computer is necessary. You may use one of the financial system programs, such as Quicken®, QuickBooks® or a even a simple Microsoft®-Excel spreadsheet. Just be sure that your income and expenses are clearly recorded and that you document the proof of payment and their purpose.

If you are an employee, any personal finance software will serve your needs. A simple Google or Bing search will offer many options with varying features and prices, usually $20-60. Some allow you to set up a budget and show you a monthly or annual comparison. Some of these personal financial software packages will keep a simplified track of income and expense file for the self-employed.

If you are self-employed, and have a fairly complex business return with inventory, invoicing, etc., I recommend using one of the business program such as QuickBooks®, MYOB®, or one of the free options.

Spreadsheet Example

You might total your monthly receipts by category and post onto a 13-column tablet or post the same in a Microsoft® Excel spreadsheet. If you do not keep the receipts together by expense category, at the end of the year someone will have to sort them by category and add them up to get the sum of each expense. Annual totals are entered on the tax return by category, not by month.

Below, I offer an abbreviated example of a spreadsheet that can be prepared in a spreadsheet or on a 13-column paper worksheet. It has a list of income and expenses in categories down the first column and monthly columns across the rest of the page. The 13th column is for annual totals.

	Jan	Feb	Mar	Apr	Nov	Dec	Tot
Income	700	700	750	800	0	400	3350
Campsite	220	220	220	220	0	100	980
Business	0	0	0	0	25	0	25
Phone	20	20	20	20	20	20	120
Internet	25	25	25	25	25	25	150
Postage	0	0	0	46	0	0	46
Parking	0	0	0	0	10	0	10
Office	25	5	10	0	0	35	75
Repairs	0	0	0	0	0	0	0
Utilities							0
Elec-							0
Gas							0
Water							0
Total	290	270	275	311	-80	180	1406
Net Inc	410	430	475	489	-80	220	1944

I have prepared a full <u>workbook</u> version of the spreadsheet with a column of rows down the left side with various categories of income and expenses on the first worksheet. Column across the top are for the 12 months of the year and a yearly total of each category down the right side. The sum of the category totals at the bottom right corner will give you a net income for the year.

Subsequent worksheets are for each category and you may post your expenses for each category worksheet by month. The total for each category worksheet will transfer automatically, by formula to the front worksheet to give you a running income and expense statement each month. The categories may be renamed to fit your needs and your particular expense needs. It works best for simple Schedule C businesses but may be adapted for employee business expenses, reported on Form 2106. You may need to study the use of spreadsheets to manipulate the pages without accidentally deleting or altering the formula.

I have posted a copy of this workbook on my blog web site: www.RVTaxMaster.com. There also is a copy on the Workamper® News website for all their members to use. If you are a Workamper® News subscriber, you may access their website and download the file at:

www.workamper.com/rvtaxmaster/incomeandexpenses.xlsx

At the minimum, you should keep your receipts in an accordion-style file folder. Label each division with your expense categories: Auto expenses, lot rentals and campground fees, utilities, turnpike / ferry tolls, and meals in route to your job assignment, office supplies, resumes, and miscellaneous. Each of the receipts should be marked as to the purpose and circumstances of the expense.

If you have a home base and are entitled to deduct the away-from-home expenses, then you should also keep a separate category for lot rent or campground fees and utilities, meals eaten out/groceries, and auto fuel while on the job. Be sure that you keep the job search deductions separate from the on the job and away-from-home deductions.

Vehicle Mileage Log

You may deduct your motorhome or truck expenses for getting to your job assignments. You may also deduct your auto/truck expenses when you use your vehicle for your employer's benefit.

For instance, if you have to drive your personal vehicle to do employer errands such as going into town to pickup mail, supplies, to drive around the campground, and other duties. These are called "vicilesnity miles" to distinguish them from "travel miles." Each are deductible but for different reasons and under different tax codes. If you have a home base and are entitled to deduct the away-from-home expenses, then keep track of your personal miles. They are deductible also, but only if you are away from home.

You must keep an accurate log of all mileage if you want to deduct any auto expenses. The auto log is how you document your business mileage, travel, vicinity, away-from-home, commuting and personal mileage. The sum of these mileage categories is your total mileage. The percentage of use in each of the categories is used to determine the deductible portion of your total auto/truck expense.

You are allowed to deduct either a percentage of your actual expenses plus the same percentage of depreciation of the vehicle or you may deduct the standard mileage rate. The IRS sets the standard mileage rate according to COLA (the Cost of Living Adjustment) and it changes each year. It was .555 per mile for 2012 and is .565 for 2013. Whichever method is best for you is generally chosen the first year a vehicle is used. Once all of your expenses are assembled and both ways are calculated, a method may be selected. The method used the first year that a vehicle is used, must generally be used throughout the time that you have and use that vehicle.

Work and Travel Diary

Many of the expenses you may deduct are for job search and away-from-home expenses. IRS Publication 463, Travel, Entertainment, Gift, and Car Expenses, (page 3), says that if you are an itinerate worker, you have no permanent home, or you take your home with you, that you may not claim any travel expenses. The expenses they are referring in that passage are away-from-home expenses.

IRS Publication 529, Miscellaneous Deductions, discusses employee business expenses and any expense you would incur in seeking work. They require the following:

1. You must be searching for work in your customary occupation.
2. You must not have a substantial break between the ending of your last job and looking for a new one.
3. You must not be looking for a job for the first time.

Since the search or travel to a prospective job, is imperative to being able to deduct your expenses, you should keep a diary or log of all of your searches showing the date that you began the search, who was contacted, and the outcome of that discussion. Keep a copy of your resume to show the type of job that you are seeking and how the new job is in that same field. Try to keep the description of your past occupation broad and the description of the job that you are seeking broad and general. You will want them as similar as possible.

Along with the purpose of the trip, list the date that you leave for the job, keep track of your vehicle mileage, and the expenses of the trip: fuel, campsites and meals. Record in you diary/log other related expenses for resumes, professional help in preparing resumes, uniforms and their cleaning, employment or job placement fees, and publications designed exclusively for job listing and assistance in the job search.

The purpose of this diary / log is to document your job search and prove the purpose of the trip is primarily for seeking employment in your usual occupation.

Verify Your Earnings

You should keep all of your time sheets, pay vouchers, and check stubs. These documents show the hours that you worked, what you were paid, and the taxes (and other withholdings) that were taken from your pay. Most employers, particularly the larger companies using a national payroll preparation services, are accurate in their math calculations. However, smaller businesses, especially those with a manual system, are prone to errors. It is always a good idea to check the math for the hours you worked, your rate of pay, and withholdings.

Match the totals of your pay stubs with the totals on your W-2 or 1099 received at the end of the year to ensure that those totals are correct. Mistakes do happen. When I worked for an accounting firm in Houston, Texas, I found an error on my own W-2. My employer had to re-issue my W-2. The following year when verifying my reported earning to the Social Security Administration, I found that the correction was not reported to them, resulting in a $4,000 difference in credits toward my earnings.

While preparing tax returns during the last 35 years, I found that some of these "mistakes" seemed intentional. In two such cases, I believe the employers inflated the 1099 earnings of a contractor to increase their own business deductions.

Fortunately, in both cases my clients had copies of their weekly pay stubs and were able to show the correct figures. It took copies of all paychecks, all earning statements, and deposit slips to prove to the Internal Revenue Service that the 1099 earnings statements, as issued, were incorrect, so my clients did not have to pay additional taxes.

How Long To Keep Tax Documents?

After you have filed your tax return, you should review your files and purge some of the unnecessary paperwork. But, how long should you keep your records? Copies of the tax returns themselves should be kept indefinitely. They are a valuable as proof of filing, of social security earnings, and as a record of reinvested dividends, and can be a source of the tax basis for various assets. Replacement copies can be obtained from the Internal Revenue Service. But, at a cost of $57 for each year, they're not cheap. In addition, the IRS does not keep all returns longer than 4 or 5 years.

The documents that support the information on your returns have somewhat shorter time requirements. The purpose of keeping these items is to substantiate the income and deductions on your return in case of a potential IRS audit or examination.

Three-Year Limit – Deductions

As long as your return does not involve fraud, tax evasion, or a substantial understatement of income, the IRS only has three years to ask you for supporting documents or proof regarding the deductions on your return. You could safeguard yourself against a potential IRS audit and keep everything if in doubt. Even if you are a minimalist, storing at the receipts of all deductions will keep the hassle of an audit at a minimum.

Cancelled checks, invoices, statements, and receipts for charities or business expenses will prove your deductions. Your interest and dividend incomes are reported to you, and to the IRS, on a 1099-Int and a 1099-Div. These should be kept for at least 3 years after your return is due or filed including extensions. Financial brokerage house statements should be kept longer because they contain information about the purchase, and thus, the basis of stock purchases. Retain them for at least 3 years after the investment is sold.

Your mortgage interest paid is reported on a 1098 if it is a qualified real estate mortgage with the house held as collateral. Those of us with RVs have a different situation. Since there is no real estate mortgage involved, a 1098 is not sent to you. Sometimes, but not always, banks or credit unions will send out a year-end summary of your interest paid that may be used as proof of your home interest.

Sometimes an RV or house is purchased on a note held by an individual. You should receive an amortization schedule showing the interest and principle payments each month and the principle balance after each payment. These will usually show the total interest and principle that was paid throughout each year. They should also show the name and mailing address of the lien holder. These should be kept for at least three years after that year's tax return is due or filed, whichever date comes later.

Seven-Year Limit - Income

If the IRS should suspect that significant income has been under reported, the statute of limitations is seven years. The IRS Code does not define clearly how much is "significant under reporting" is. Sometimes this can be simply the results of an overlooked deposit form an annuity or some other non-recurring event. Sometimes it can happen if under audit the IRS should find a greater sum of bank deposits than is reflected by your tax return. If you deposit significant, non-taxable income but do not show from what source it came from.

Un-Limited – Fraud or Non-Filing

If they suspect fraud, then the statute of limitation never runs out. Fraud is defined as a willfully and knowingly under reporting income or claiming obviously incorrect deductions. If a tax return is never filed, the statue's time never starts; so, the limit for the IRS to come after you for an unfiled return never ends.

Receipts for property improvements to home, rental, or business property, or other investments could affect your return many years after the purchase. These receipts should be kept for at least seven years past the year the property is sold.

In general, these guidelines cover only a select overview of the type of documents you should keep. For more information on record keeping, you can review IRS Publication 552 "Record Keeping for Individuals." You may find this publication on the government's website irs.gov and print it or download and save it on your computer.

[10]

Need To File Multi-State Income Tax Returns?

Non-Resident Returns

Most people are familiar with filing federal 1040 returns and the state returns for their resident state. Many have been required to file a couple of state returns in one year when they have moved to a new state during the year. Usually these are filed as "part-year residents" in one state the first half of the year and one in the second state for the last half of the year.

If you are a resident of one state, whether you have a home base or are a full-time traveler, and travel to another state to work, your W-2 will be mailed to your home address or mail forwarding service. But, it will show the wages as being paid in the temporary work state and taxes will be withheld for the work state.

Generally, you will file the out-of-state return first and pay any additional tax or claim a refund for that state. Then file your home state taxes claiming the out-of-state earnings and a credit for the taxes paid on the out-of-state return.

Some states will want all of a non-resident's income reported, the same as reported on the Federal 1040. Taxes are calculated on all income as if you were a resident of that state. These states will have a schedule to separate the income that was earned within their state from the total income. The percentage of their state income to the total federal income is the percentage that is applied to the total tax.

The reason states calculate tax using this method is that it gets small, short-term earnings raised into a higher tax bracket. This method was pioneered in the State of Kansas 25 years ago. I have watched this method spread to other states as the economy has encouraged state governments to tighten their belts and look for new ways to increase revenue without having to raise tax rates.

If your earnings in a non-resident state are minimal (under $1,000 or $2,000), there may not be a need to file a return for that state if enough taxes were withheld to satisfy that state auditor's anticipated tax liability. This rule is not consistent across all of the many states. Each has varying rules and if you have a significant amount of state taxes withheld you might want to file, even if there is no tax liability, to get any tax money withheld returned to you.

Nine states do not use state income tax as a revenue method. Those states are Alaska, Florida, Nevada, New Hampshire, South Dakota, Tennessee, Texas, Washington and Wyoming. Two of those states

(Tennessee and New Hampshire) do have a tax on intangibles, interest, and dividend accounts.

That leaves 41 states that do have a state income tax, with 41 different methods of calculating those taxes. Even those methods that seem similar have differences. For instance, some states do not tax retirement pensions and others give a moderate-to-large exemption for retirement pensions. Some states do not have a very large tax rate, 1-3%, while others range as high as 7-11% plus adding another 3-10% for a local or municipality tax.

Choosing a Domicile

Most RVers will move to Texas, Florida, or one of the nine states that do not have an income tax to avoid a state income tax, particularly on a retirement pension. However, I suggest that you look at what the tax rates are in the various states, along with other factors that are worth considering. *"Choosing Your RV Home Base"* published by Roundabout

Publications (and listed on the Workamper® News website bookstore) has an excellent listing of the useful state facts, including state and local taxes, sales taxes, vehicle registration, emission/safety testing, cost of living indicators, and weather items. In the context used by the writers of this book, the term "home base" does not mean the brick/stick structure that we use but merely a base from which to travel. They mean the same as a residential state or a domicile.

You should also check with a prospective state's insurance board to verify auto and/or real estate insurance rates. A high insurance rate caused by careless driving habits, can negate the savings of a low state income tax. The same is true for real estate property taxes.

[11]

How & Where Are They Deducted?

Where your expenses are deducted depends on whether you are an employee or an independent contractor. If you are an employee, they are considered employee business expenses. If you have only a few deductions with relatively a small total amount, they may be deducted directly on Schedule A, under the "Subject to 2% of AGI" limitation. That means 2% of your Adjusted Gross Income (the bottom line on the front page of the 1040) is deducted first, commonly called the "2% haircut." Anything over that 2% may be counted as a deduction.

If you have several items and a substantial total amount in deductions, or if you have depreciation on your vehicle or other assets, you must then use IRS Form 2106 Employee Business Expenses. That form will list all of your expenses with various limitations and then summarize the total at the bottom. The results will be listed on the Schedule A on the 2% subject line and your income is listed with as a W-2 on line 7 of the 1040.

If you are an independent contractor, your income and expenses are listed on a Schedule C and there is no 2% AGI limit to your expenses. Any depreciation of business assets is deducted here and your net income is subject to a self-employment tax calculation. Your net income is not reduced by the standard deduction, itemized deductions, or by the personal exemption. At this point the Self-Employment tax is calculated. Then the net income is carried to the front page of the Form 1040 to be added with other income and losses.

The self-employment tax is charged to self-employed individuals in lieu of Social Security taxes being withheld by an employer. Half of the self-employment tax is deducted on the front page of the 1040 as an adjustment to income. There are other adjustments listed there such as an IRA and self-employed health insurance, hence the net result is called "Adjusted Gross Income."

Employees whose job search expenses are deducted on Schedule A, line 21 Employee Business Expenses, are limited by 2% of Adjusted Gross Income. Many times the taxpayer's income is high enough that the 2% limitation wipes out the deduction. Other times the deduction may be larger than the 2% of AGI but the total itemized deductions are not greater than the standard deduction. In these cases, job search deductions do not help.

Below is a table showing a couple of income levels and the effect it has on the employee business expense deduction. Because of the higher income in the second column and the higher AGI, the employee business expense deduction is wiped out and does not benefit the taxpayer. Also, if the total itemized deductions were less because there were no medical expenses, then the standard deduction would be the greater and business expenses should not be used.

Example: Itemized deductions at different income levels:

	AGI 40,000	AGI $150,000	Std Ded
Net Medical		1,200	
Taxes		3,000	
Mortgage Inter-est	6,000	6,000	
Donations	1,200	1,200	
Misc: Empl Bus Exp	1,200	3,000	
Less 2% of AGI	3,000	-3,000	
Net Misc Deductions	2,200	-0-	
Total Item Deduction	13,600	11,400	11,900

Note that self-employment income is reported as a net figure on the front page of the return, above the AGI. There is no reason to worry about having more than the standard deduction, since it will always be deducted above the AGI.

If you have elected a separate entity for your business, such as a partnership, S corporation, or limited liability company, a separate tax return is prepared with a Form K-1 for each partner or shareholder to reflect their proportion of the income. That income is reported on a Schedule E, page 2.

If you have selected a corporate business structure, without a Sub-Chapter S election, then a separate corporate tax return is prepared and the corporation pays its own income tax.

[12]

Do You Have A Business or Hobby?

Many RVers have small, sideline businesses that they operate from their rig as they travel from one employed job to another. After all, what better tax shelter is there than a Schedule C business that loses money all the time?

We are always told that it is best to have tax deductions above the AGI, but the IRS considers a Schedule C business that continually lose money to be a hobby. If the "business" is not conducted with a sincere profit motive and does not observe proper business procedures, then it is assumed to be solely for personal pleasure, in other words a hobby.

The IRS presumes that an activity is conducted for profit if it makes a profit during at least three of the last five years, including the current year. For all of you RVers who are equestrian fans, there must be a profit for at least two of the last seven years for activities that consist primarily of breeding, showing, training or racing horses.

To make a determination of whether an individual is engaged an activity for profit, the IRS considers:

1. Does the time and effort put into the activity indicate a profit?
2. Is there a dependence on income from the activity?
3. Is the loss due to circumstances beyond the taxpayer's control or from the start-up phase?
4. Has the taxpayer changed methods of operation to improve profitability?
5. Does the taxpayer have the knowledge needed to conduct this business or, if not, has he sought worthy advisors?

6. Has the taxpayer made a profit in similar activities in the past?

7. Does the activity make a profit in some years?

8. Can the taxpayer expect to make a profit in the future in the appreciation of assets when sold?

If the IRS deems the business to be a hobby, they will report the income on the front page of the 1040, Line 21 – Miscellaneous Income. The expenses are deducted however, on Schedule A-Misc. Deductions are subject to the 2% of AGI haircut. If you do not have enough other Schedule A deductions from medical, taxes, and charitable donations to be greater than the standard deduction, then you lose the deductions for that year. However, the income is still taxable and it raises the AGI and thus reduces the allowed Miscellaneous Deductions.

A key factor in this determination is whether the taxpayer has intent to make a profit and whether they have a written business plan.

I have worked with clients in the past who were challenged by the IRS for not showing a profit within the required number of years. Two were auto-racing activities; one was a landscape photographer. The IRS thought the activities were just hobbies. After much discussion with the auditors and showing the client records, we were able to prove that the activities were conducted in a businesslike manner and were allowed to continue even though they did not meet the 3 out of 5 profitable years.

These clients kept meticulous records of their business with a separate checking account, and printed monthly or quarterly financial statements. They knew all about auto racing, tuning the car, and driving at high speeds on a crowded racetrack. What they did not know was how to measure their business successes or losses beyond whether they won or lost races.

I helped them to devise a business plan, and guided them in not just keeping their own records, but also in monitoring those records. Together, we would review their records to see where they were wasting money and to make projections for the coming season.

Their business plan showed that they did not have to be the winner of each race. Sure, they would get prize money, but their main source of income was sponsorships. A large check from the advertising department of Hertz or Budweiser can go a long way toward paying bills and showing a profit. All that they had to do was be up in the crowd of cars at the finish lap and have a car that would stand out. Fan viewership was what the sponsors looked for. Consider Danica Patrick and her bright, lime-green NASCAR racecar. It stands out in the crowd.

If you have a reasonably written business plan and have an intention to make a profit, you have a profit motive. It is very difficult for the IRS to win in examination, appeals or tax court if you can demonstrate that you do have a sincere intent and a profit motive no matter how unlikely it may be.

[13]

Example of A Part-Timer With Home Base & High Itemized Deductions?

Background

Carl and Joyce are a couple in their mid 50s, that travel frequently in their motorhome. Carl had been a millwright, but was laid off after 18 years with the same factory when the business closed. Joyce worked at a minimum wage job to support them for a year until Carl got a new job as a millwright work-ing for a contractor building large factory installa-tions. The trouble was the job took him around the country to different sites for 5-7 months at a time. With the overtime pay, he made a great deal more

125

than he had been earning, so Joyce quit her minimum pay job to travel with him. The housing market was not particularly great in their area, so they kept the house. They liked the house and neighborhood, they owned their house without a mortgage, and eventually wanted to retire there. They kept the utilities on so a neighbor could come over and mow the lawn and look after the house.

The motorhome, which they had been using for vacations, now became their home away from home. They came back to their house to live during stretches between jobs and during the Thanksgiving and Christmas holidays. They have enough mortgage interest on the motorhome as well as the real estate property taxes and state income taxes, that they can claim itemized deductions rather than taking the standard deduction.

Analysis

Because their living expenses are duplicated while they are working away from home, they can deduct all of their campground fees, utilities, and half of their groceries and Carl's meals when they dine out. If Joyce were to work some place while Carl was working on the construction site, her part of the groceries and her dining out might be deductable also. I say "might be" because her working wasn't the intended purpose for the trip. To me, that is a gray area of the tax code and depends on when the decisions were made for Joyce to make the trip, her purpose for the trip, and whether she would be working. These decisions and the timing should be well documented in their travel diary.

Carl tows a little pickup behind the motorhome. He uses it for personal use and commuting to the construction site. The personal use is usually not deductible but because he is on a temporary job and considered away-from-home, he may deduct the commuting portion of his truck. Because they are away-from-home and the motorhome is no longer used for vacations, they may depreciate the motorhome, deduct all of the maintenance, and fuel costs.

If Carl's employer were to reimburse him for his travel expenses or just pay him an unaccountable travel allowance, then Carl must report that as income on the IRS Form 2106: Employee Business Expenses. That might reduce his deduction to the point that it is less than the 2% of Adjusted Gross Income.

[14]

Example of Part-timer With Home Base and Standard Deduction

Background

Vernon and Carol had both worked at various jobs throughout their lives, none of which had good retirement plans if any. When they each retired at age 66, they had little in their 401k plans and even less in their IRAs. They were not big savers. But, they were thrifty and could live economically. They decided that they could live on their combined monthly Social Security and not touch their retirement funds if they both continued to work at least part-time to supplement their income. Their house in South Texas was paid for and required minimal upkeep.

They decided that rather than stay at home and work, they would use Workamper® News to see what jobs they could find in other parts of the country. They bought a small travel trailer that could be pulled behind their SUV. They then attended a Workamper® networking conference in Arkansas where they obtained help in drafting resumes and met with representatives from one of the concessionaires. They both found jobs working at the Grand Canyon during the summer and for a wild life preserve in South Texas during the winter. The wild life preserve was only twenty miles from their home. They could live at home and not have to take the RV.

Vernon's past work experience had been in retail sales work and Carol had always worked various clerical duties in a variety of offices. Vernon was to work in the souvenir store and Carol was to keep the time sheets in the office for the concessioner.

These jobs were similar to occupations they held previously, so the job search and travel expenses to the Grand Canyon were deductible. The expenses they incurred going to the Workamper® News Rendezvous, their expenses networking with other RVers to seek Workamper type jobs, and having resumes prepared were also deductible.

Analysis

Because they are duplicating their living expenses while they are working at the Grand Canyon, the cost of the travel trailer and their utilities are deductable. They are entitled to deduct all of these expenses; however, since they don't spend much for travel and their home is paid for, they don't have enough itemized deductions to be greater than the standard deduction. Thus, the tracking all of their Workamper travel and job search expenses probably will not have an impact on their return even though they are entitled to deduct them.

I would recommend they still keep track of these expenses for at least the first couple of years. Even though they do not have any mortgage interest on their home or RV and are expecting to claim the standard deduction, their travel expenses and employee deductions could have a greater impact in future years and they may qualify for claiming larger itemized deductions in the future.

Still, they are working only seasonally and their earnings will not be over $18,000. Their Social Security Benefit is not taxable (in this case). So, after the standard deduction and personal exemptions, they do not expected to have any tax liability, anyway.

[15]

Example of Full-timer With Itemized Deductions

Background

Ed and Linda retired somewhat early. Ed retired from General Motors when they offered management staff an early retirement package. He converted his considerable retirement settlement to an annuity and immediately started drawing. Linda had been mostly a stay at home mom, but had worked outside the house for the last couple of years. She had no retirement provisions other than the IRA account Ed had started for her. Their kids were out of the house, on their own, and financially secure.

With Ed's comfortable salary and a now comfortable pension, they were used to living well with all of the toys that made their lives enjoyable.

Their big house now felt like a cavern with the kids gone. It was not the house that they wanted to live in forever. It had been purchased to be big enough to raise their family. After devoting their lives to raising kids, they wanted time to themselves, and the opportunity to finally do the things that they had always wanted to do.

They decided to buy a motorhome and travel the country sightseeing, playing golf, and enjoying their new life and freedom. It was to be a second honeymoon. They sold their house when the market was fair. They bought a Prevost motorhome, a big 40' one, and a new SUV to tow behind it. They did not want to be bored, so they looked into volunteering for Habitat for Humanity but first they wanted to see the Redwood Forest and Yellowstone National Park. After contacting the park service, they accepted a job at one of the gates taking tickets. They would only have to work 8 hours each per week in exchange for a campsite and utilities. They played a lot of golf at a nearby course in their spare time.

Analysis

With the high interest paid on their motorhome, and the high state income taxes they paid, Ed and Linda will probably always be able to claim the larger itemized deductions. Their trip to California to see the Redwood Forest is considered a trip for a non-profit organization – a federal agency in this case. Thus, their costs could be deducted as a charitable donation. The campground site that was furnished as a work-required fringe benefit and is not considered taxable income. If the campground fees were reported as income, they could be deducted as a charitable donation.

These donations only work if the organization is a qualified, not-for-profit organization or a state or national governmental agency. Non-profit organizations usually do not issue a W-2 or 1099.

Some "for-profit" companies furnish a campsite but do not require any other services. However you are required to stay there. That is a condition of the job. Contracting companies do this frequently at a construction site. It is cheaper for them and they have someone there for security at night. Since it is a requirement for the job, it also is a non-taxable benefit.

However, if Ed and Linda were to work for a for-profit business, their purposes might not be considered as having a "profit" motive, but merely to secure a place so they could play golf, a personal pleasure. If their purpose is not to make money, the whole activity could be construed as taxable to them, particularly if the business were to issue them a W-2 or 1099. Their travel expenses may not be deductible if the campground is not a qualified not-profit organization or they do not have an earning intent other than just a place to stay.

[16]

Example of Full-timer With Standard Deductions

Background

Jerry had been a schoolteacher for 24 years. He was nearing retirement when his wife of 25 years decided she wanted to be single again. Jerry was crushed. He did not know what he would do. They had no longer had children at home. Their daughter was married but with no children of her own yet. Their son was in his last year of college and had a position already lined up with a bank upon graduation.

As a property settlement of their divorce, Jerry's wife got the house along with the mortgage. Jerry got to keep his school retirement plan, which he could start withdrawing in a few years. Jerry decided to quit teaching, purchase a motorhome, and see, first-hand, some of the U.S. geography he had been teaching for so many years. He would start drawing his teacher retirement in 5 years.

He financed a small Class C motorhome and found that his little Mazda car could be towed behind it on a dolly. Since it was several years old, the mortgage was very small, but it was in good condition and well cared for, and thus, quite reliable.

He had enough in savings, along with the proceeds from selling his fishing boat, to support himself for a year. Although he did not have to work, he thought he might -- if he found the perfect opportunity. Jerry was now as free as a bird!

That fall his life changed. Instead of preparing for the next school term, with his days filled with laying out lesson plans and learning the new state requirements for a stricter curriculum, his biggest decision became where he should stop the motorhome for the night. He drove toward New England, hoping to get there before the foliage turned. He had read about the beauty of this time of year in this historic part of our country, but had never been able to experience it.

He had always wanted to write something: a short story, a novel, a book of some kind, but never felt he had the time or life experience to write it. He would get that now. His first couple of nights were spent in the parking lot of a large shopping center. He parked along the outer edge so he would not disturb the customer traffic flow. Since his motorhome was self-contained, he had plenty of fresh water and almost empty holding tanks, he felt that he could stay overnight and still maintain the sanctity of the area. He visited a restaurant in the shopping center for supper then a grocery store for items for his pantry.

When Jerry spent the night in a shopping center, he returned the favor of the overnight stay by patronizing the businesses there. He kept a low profile, parked on the perimeter of the parking lot, did not extend the awnings or put down the leveling leg, and only spent one night at any shopping center. He was only passing through.

After spending several weeks in New England, Jerry was at an RV campground visiting with the owner. The owner lamented the loss of a summer employee who decided to leave the job early before the end of the season and before his contract ended. "You just can't get good help anymore," he complained. Jerry asked what the duties were and asked whether he would be a suitable replacement.

Jerry stayed several weeks, long after the season ended to help the owner clean the campground and prepare it for the winter. He was paid as an employee and was asked to return next spring. Jerry said he would consider it. He was not sure about his future, but he had enjoyed his weeks at the campground. He enjoyed the leisurely work, the freedom from the pressure of the school district's restrictions. He had already started getting some possible story ideas.

Analysis

Because Jerry's trip to New England was primarily for personal enjoyment and because he was not searching for work on his way there, the costs of this trip cannot be considered a deduction. In addition, since any of the jobs that he might have done at this campground could not be considered in the same line of work that he had been doing as a teacher, this was purely a personal, non-deductible trip. But, Jerry has minimal interest expense on his motorhome, so he doesn't have enough to be able to claim the Schedule A itemized deductions. So, even if the trip were deductible, it would not have mattered. The employee business expenses, the job search, and the trip combined were not even close to the standard deduction of $5,950.

For Jerry, that did not matter. Since his income was not sizeable, taking the standard deduction and personal exemption left him with taxable income of less than $2000 and a federal tax bill of less than $200, while his state income tax was under $50.

Jerry wanted freedom away from cares and worries. He was on a sabbatical, free from his past structured life.

Let us change the story a little, now. Let us say that Jerry had not been a classroom instructor, but a school administrator and that he was at retirement age. Let us, also, say that his income before he retired was $65,000 per year plus health insurance coverage. Now his income is significant. After the standard deduction and personal exemption, his taxable income would be $55,250. His tax due on federal taxes alone would be $4975! That does not even consider state tax liability.

I do not know about you, but that gets my attention. It is worthwhile to try to lower that tax liability. Of course, with that much of salary and pension, he could have approximately $6,000 of Federal income tax withheld which would give him a $1,025 refund. Still, that is a lot of money to "leave on the table" for our government to waste.

I do not think that there is anything that Jerry can do about this year as presented. If he had given more thought to his plans, he might signed up with Workamper® News, attended a Rendezvous networking conference prior making his trip, and maybe he could have justified some of his expenses as legitimate job seeking expenses. Still, with only the standard deduction, it would not have made any difference.

Going forward, if he were to return to Vermont the next year and work at the same RV campground, it would now be in the line of work he was now doing. He would have the purpose of returning to a job, so expenses all would now be deductible.

He is still an itinerate worker with no home base. He still will not be eligible for any away-from-home expense deductions. With minimal health costs (health insurance paid for by the school retirement system) and minimal mortgage insurance, he probably will not have much to itemize, so he will still use the standard deduction.

He needs to start a self-employment business. Maybe he can get his book started. If it were a best seller though, he would have an even bigger tax problem. But, wouldn't that be a nice problem to have? Steven Spielberg may want to make a movie out of it and make an even bigger, even nicer, tax problem!

[17]

Example of Self Employed Full-timer With Standard Deductions

Background

Troy and Melissa were a young corporate couple in their 30s. They had been married for 5 years and had one son, Billy, age four. Troy was a mechanical engineer for a company that built automated conveyor systems for factories. Melissa was a graphic artist who maintained the Internet presence for a large company.

Troy and Melissa felt that their busy lives in the corporate world were taking too much of their time from raising Billy. His little personality was being shaped too much by daycare centers, even though Troy and Melissa carefully scrutinized each one. There was not any alternative they liked. They considered moving to another city but it would require them both to change jobs.

They decided to do something radical, instead. They sold their condominium and one of the cars; bought a small 5th wheel trailer that could be towed by Troy's pickup and started their own businesses. Now, they could move to any place they wanted with Billy. They had enough in savings to support themselves for a few months while they got their businesses started and they could get part-time jobs until the businesses could support them.

Troy had been interested in solar energy for several years. He thought it was the solution to our nations' dependence on foreign oil. He contacted a company in Scottsdale, AZ about wholesaling him solar panels. The panels could be mounted on RVs to provide electrical power to re-charge deep-cycle batteries. Solar panels, when configured properly, allow an RVer to stay off the grid, unconnected except for a weekly or bi-weekly stop to refill the fresh water tanks and to dump the holding tanks. He also found a wholesale source for wind generators that could be mounted on RVs for additional energy and a wholesale source for solar ovens.

Melissa started a business helping their campground neighbors to clean up their computers and to resolve their Microsoft® Windows issues. She eventually set up a website to sell products on the Internet that could be drop-shipped directly to the customer. They could travel whenever the changes in the climate were not to their liking. Although Billy was only 4, they had already started him on a curriculum for home schooling.

The 5th wheel had a shop compartment in the back, a toy hauler, for Troy's work. Occasionally, they stayed at RV campgrounds so Troy could promote his solar energy business. A lot of his business came from Internet connections and through friends in the

Escapees Boomer network. He could sit out in the desert on Bureau Land Management land and meet with his friends and install newly purchased solar panels ordered for his customers. He had the panels shipped to the nearest UPS outlet. BLM land is empty, unused government land that is being held for future use. Any one may camp on the lane for two weeks at a time as long as they do not disturb the fauna, wildlife or violate certain other rules.

Since Melissa's Internet sales are shipped to her customers for her by the wholesaler, she does not have to be in any particular place to conduct her businesses. With all of Melissa's sales coming from the Internet with a mailing address in Las Vegas and a Nevada residency, all of her sales are subject to Nevada state income reporting.

Analysis

Because Troy and Melissa do not have a brick and stick home anywhere, they are itinerate workers. Both their home and tax home is where ever they are at any given moment. They are residents of Nevada because they spend more of their time there in summer and winter, when it is not too hot or too cold. Their vehicles are registered there as well as their driver's licenses and their voter registrations.

They are never away-from-home, so they are not eligible to deduct any of their campground expenses. The shop part of the 5th wheel trailer qualifies as an "office in the home" deduction on Troy's Schedule C. Melissa's business is operated on the laptop computer from the dinette table when they are not having meals. She shares the computer with Billy, who uses it for his home schooling.

Since Melissa's office space is not exclusively used for her business and the computer is used partly for personal use, she can only deduct the cost of her website and postage for her Schedule C business.

Both of them are self-employed and report all their income on Schedule Cs. Whether they have enough employee business expenses to qualify more that the 2% of AGI, and enough itemized deductions to claim more than standard deduction, is not an issue for them.

[18]

Summary & My Point Of View

Purpose

The reason I have written this book is to share my experiences while I traveled the USA and lived in a motorhome. My wife and I enjoyed it very much; we felt that it was one of the most relaxing, stimulating, and enlightening times of our lives. I would like to help those RVers who want to do the same.

I have met many RVers who were worried about their tax liability. Some were concerned because they did not understand the complicated procedure of filing multi-state income tax returns. It is the big unknown for many working RVers. There are so

151

many states and so many different rules. They had heard many disastrous tales from others -- some true, some not, some partially and some still unresolved.

Like many of us, some RVers are concerned about the proper payment of federal and state income taxes. This is good. Individuals should be conscious of the amount of taxes they have to pay and should plan and structure their lives in order to pay as little as possible.

A few, however, are willing to go to such great lengths to avoid paying any at all, that they lose sight of a more important goal: reducing money outflow overall. They are willing to spend large sums of money just to save paying a little income tax. That is being penny-wise and pound-foolish.

Each situation is different, sometimes travel expenses are deductible, and sometimes they are not. A lot depends on how the deduction is justified beforehand and how well it is documented afterwards. The planning, recording and documenting are the key to saving your tax dollars.

Viewpoint

If you have a home that you want to keep to return to some day when you are though RVing, should that day ever come, fine. Keep the house. Rent it out, or do whatever you feel is necessary to keep your cash outflow at an acceptable level.

You might want to come back to the home to rest between "tours" or excursions. Maybe you want to raise a vegetable or flower garden. Perhaps you want a place to brew your own beer or make your own wine on occasion. (That is very hard to do in an RV although I met a man who did it.)

However, if you just want to have the house so that you can say that you have a home base and you want to deduct your away-from-home expenses, save yourself time and money. Sell the house and do not duplicate the expense just to save a little on taxes. The taxes saved by deducting the away-from-home travel expenses are not nearly as much as the cost of keeping the home in the first place.

What is most important is to get out of debt: credit cards, vehicles, RV and, yes, the home if you still have it. I have heard folks respond: "But, I'll have to pay a lot of income taxes without the home interest deduction!" Yes, you will have to pay more income tax, but not nearly as much as you will save by eliminating the house payment, homeowner's insurance, property taxes, utilities and the maintenance costs.

I was surprised how little Charisse and I needed to live when we were traveling in the RV with no home base. We still kept our credit cards. Charisse had one for her personal use and I had two: one for personal use and one for business. Each of these cards were paid off in full at the end of the billing cycle.

What is important is to minimize your cash outflow until you can live below your means, not just within it. That is why I recommend if you are going to live the RV lifestyle and work while you travel in your RV, sell the home. Do not worry about trying to keep a home base just for the tax deductions.

If you do want to keep the house and eventually return to it, then here are the tax deductions that you can take if you keep a detailed diary of your work assignments, searches, and travel.

Open a savings account and have a good portion of your income deposited there. You might have all of your income deposited there and only withdraw monthly what you will need for that month's living expenses. You will discover that as you build your savings, you will have the cash you need to pay for emergency expenses. You will even have cash to spend on occasional, well planned "luxury" items.

Being debt-free and having money in the bank gives you the wonderful feeling of being in control of your life and finances; and hope that, at some point, you will not have to work and will be able to live off your investments. That is called wealth. "It is not the man who has too little, but the man who craves more, that is poor." Seneca the Younger, Roman Philosopher, ca 4 BC -65 AD.

What is not important is accumulating things. Things that comedian George Carlin used to talk about, your "stuff." Stuff is what you keep in the house that you want to return to someday...maybe. Stuff is what you pay a monthly storage fee for, back in some city that you have long forgotten (but the rent keeps being drafted from your bank account). Sure, you may have some family possessions and heirlooms you want to pass on to your own heirs. Could you just distribute those now?

Charisse and I had such treasures: a stereo system complete with turntable, cassette player and am/fm radio. Remember those? We had extra pieces of furniture, pictures, and 13 boxes of books plus Grandmother's china, my Triumph Spitfire sports car and trophies. We paid $50 per month for 13 years, thinking we were going to use them someday. When we finally calculated that we had paid almost $7,800 for the luxury of that storage, we determined that most of what we had was just sentimental junk.

In 2008, when we left Kerrville, Texas to travel as full-timers again, we donated most of our extra "stuff" to a charitable organization. I drove the sports car to Orlando, Florida and presented it to my daughter and grandson. We kept Grandmother's china, though. I guess some things you just cannot get rid of; besides, it would fit it into the basement of the motorhome.

A Challenge To The Reader

My challenge to you, as a reader, is to examine your own lives and decide what direction you want to take. You are probably at that crossroads now if you contemplating the RV lifestyle or if you are already traveling and living it. Are your travels just for sightseeing this country? Do you plan to work on the road to help pay the costs? Are you living in the RV and traveling as an expression of freedom, to go where and when you want?

If you plan to work while you travel, read the entire book, even those sections that you do not think pertain to you now. You will learn a lot about the choices available to you.

I realize that some folks could not care less about taxes and certainly do not want to read about them. That is all right, we need folks like them; folks that have other skills that the rest of us do not have. For the rest of you, the ones still reading, structure your lives and family records to include a travel diary, vehicle mileage log, and all of the records of your various deductible expenses. You now know what they are.

Keep your expenses to a minimum and save what you can. Then you can work if you want to, doing what you want to do. You will no longer work merely because you have to. You can volunteer your services to projects that are dear to your heart or try your hand at ventures that you may have always wanted to try but never had the time.

Set up a budget to estimate you cash flow. Many books and websites do an excellent job of showing you how to outline a basic budget. Some are even designed especially for the RVer.

Remember, a budget is not intended to restrict you from spending your money, but to help you prioritize your spending at the beginning of the month so you have what you need and want without running out of money before the end of the month.

Finally, talk with a tax professional to determine an estimate of you tax liability before the end of the year or before you make the "big jump" to RVing so that you will have an idea of your tax liability in advance. It is always nice to have at least some idea of what is coming, whether you like the outcome or not. If your tax liability is going to be big, then you will know how to spend your money. Or, you will know how much to put aside and how much you can spend on other things. If your tax liability is not nearly as large as anticipated, you will enjoy greater peace of mind and a larger savings account!

Appendix

Numbered List

Copy of 1040, page 1

Copy of 1040, page 2

Copy of Schedule A

Copy of Form 2106, page 1

Copy of Form 2106, page 2

Copy of Schedule C

Copy of Excel Spreadsheets

Copy of Sample Auto Log

Form 1040

Department of the Treasury - Internal Revenue Service (99)

2012

U.S. Individual Income Tax Return

OMB No. 1545-0074   IRS Use Only-Do not write or staple in this space.

For the year Jan 1-Dec 31, 2012, or other tax year beginning _____ 2012, ending _____ , 20 ___

See separate instructions.

Your first name and initial	Last name	Your social security number

If a joint return, spouse's first name and initial	Last name	Spouse's social security number

Home address (number and street).	Apt. no.	▲ Make sure the SSN(s) above and on line 6c are correct.

City, town or post office, state, and ZIP code. If you have a foreign address, also complete spaces below (see instructions).

Presidential Election Campaign
Check here if you, or your spouse if filing jointly, want $3 to go to this fund. Checking a box below will not change your tax or refund.   ☐ You   ☐ Spouse

Foreign country name	Foreign province/state/county	Foreign postal code

Filing Status

Check only one box.

1. ☐ Single
2. ☐ Married filing jointly (even if only one had income)
3. ☐ Married filing separately. Enter spouse's SSN above and full name here. ▶
4. ☐ Head of household (with qualifying person). (See instructions.) If the qualifying person is a child but not your dependent, enter this child's name here. ▶
5. ☐ Qualifying widow(er) with dependent child

Exemptions

6a ☐ Yourself. If someone can claim you as a dependent, do not check box 6a . . . . }

b ☐ Spouse . . . .

Boxes checked on 6a and 6b ___
No. of children ___

c Dependents:

(1) First name Last name	(2) Dependent's social security number	(3) Dependent's relationship to you	(4) Chk if child under age 17 qualifying for child tax credit (see instructions)
			☐
			☐
			☐
			☐

If more than four dependents, see instructions and check here ▶ ☐

▶ lived with you ___
▶ did not live with you due to divorce or separation (see instructions) ___
Dependents on 6c not entered above ___
Add numbers on lines above ▶ ☐

d Total number of exemptions claimed . . . .

Income

Attach Form(s) W-2 here. Also attach Forms W-2G and 1099-R if tax was withheld.

If you did not get a W-2, see instructions.

Enclose, but do not attach, any payment. Also, please use Form 1040-V.

7	Wages, salaries, tips, etc. Attach Form(s) W-2	**7**	
8a	Taxable interest. Attach Schedule B if required	**8a**	
b	Tax-exempt interest. Do not include on line 8a	8b	
9a	Ordinary dividends. Attach Schedule B if required	**9a**	
b	Qualified dividends	9b	
10	Taxable refunds, credits, or offsets of state and local income taxes	**10**	
11	Alimony received	**11**	
12	Business income or (loss). Attach Schedule C or C-EZ	**12**	
13	Capital gain or (loss). Attach Schedule D if required. If not required, check here ▶ ☐	**13**	
14	Other gains or (losses). Attach Form 4797	**14**	
15a	IRA distributions	15a		b Taxable amount	**15b**	
16a	Pensions and annuities . .	16a		b Taxable amount	**16b**	
17	Rental real estate, royalties, partnerships, S corporations, trusts, etc. Attach Schedule E	**17**	
18	Farm income or (loss). Attach Schedule F	**18**	
19	Unemployment compensation	**19**	
20a	Social security benefits . .	20a		b Taxable amount	**20b**	
21	Other income	**21**	
22	Combine the amounts in the far right column for lines 7 through 21. This is your **total income** . . . . ▶	**22**	

Adjusted Gross Income

23	Educator expenses	23	
24	Certain business expenses of reservists, performing artists, and fee-basis government officials. Attach Form 2106 or 2106-EZ	24	
25	Health savings account deduction. Attach Form 8889 . . .	25	
26	Moving expenses. Attach Form 3903	26	
27	Deductible part of self-employment tax. Attach Schedule SE .	27	
28	Self-employed SEP, SIMPLE, and qualified plans	28	
29	Self-employed health insurance deduction	29	
30	Penalty on early withdrawal of savings	30	
31a	Alimony paid b Recipient's SSN ▶	31a	
32	IRA deduction	32	
33	Student loan interest deduction	33	
34	Tuition and fees. Attach Form 8917	34	
35	Domestic production activities deduction. Attach Form 8903 . .	35	
36	Add lines 23 through 35	**36**	
37	Subtract line 36 from line 22. This is your **adjusted gross income** . . . . ▶	**37**	

For Disclosure, Privacy Act, and Paperwork Reduction Act Notice, see separate instructions.
EEA

Form 1040 (2012)

Form 1040 (2012)

Tax and Credits	38	Amount from line 37 (adjusted gross income)		38
	39a	Check { You were born before January 2, 1948, ☐ Blind. } Total boxes if { Spouse was born before January 2, 1948, ☐ Blind. } checked ▶ 39a		
Standard Deduction for -	b	If your spouse itemizes on a separate return or you were a dual-status alien, check here ▶ 39b ☐		
● People who check any box on line 39a or 39b or who can be claimed as a dependent, see Instructions.	40	Itemized deductions (from Schedule A) or your standard deduction (see left margin)		40
	41	Subtract line 40 from line 38		41
	42	Exemptions. Multiply $3,800 by the number on line 6d		42
	43	Taxable income. Subtract line 42 from line 41. If line 42 is more than line 41, enter -0-		43
● All others:	44	Tax (see instructions). Check if any from: a ☐ Form(s) 8814 b ☐ Form 4972 c ☐ 962 election		44
Single or Married filing separately, $5,950	45	Alternative minimum tax (see instructions). Attach Form 6251		45
	46	Add lines 44 and 45 ▶		46
	47	Foreign tax credit. Attach Form 1116 if required	47	
Married filing jointly or Qualifying widow(er), $11,900	48	Credit for child and dependent care expenses. Attach Form 2441	48	
	49	Education credits from Form 8863, line 19	49	
	50	Retirement savings contributions credit. Attach Form 8880	50	
Head of household, $8,700	51	Child tax credit. Attach Schedule 8812, if required	51	
	52	Residential energy credit. Attach Form 5695	52	
	53	Other credits from Form: a ☐ 3800 b ☐ 8801 c ☐	53	
	54	Add lines 47 through 53. These are your total credits		54
	55	Subtract line 54 from line 46. If line 54 is more than line 46, enter -0- ▶		55
Other Taxes	56	Self-employment tax. Attach Schedule SE		56
	57	Unreported social security and Medicare tax from Form: a ☐ 4137 b ☐ 8919		57
	58	Additional tax on IRAs, other qualified retirement plans, etc. Attach Form 5329 if required		58
	59 a	Household employment taxes from Schedule H		59a
	b	First-time homebuyer credit repayment. Attach Form 5405 if required		59b
	60	Other taxes. Enter code(s) from instructions		60
	61	Add lines 55 through 60. This is your total tax ▶		61
Payments	62	Federal income tax withheld from Forms W-2 and 1099	62	
	63	2012 estimated tax payments and amount applied from 2011 return	63	
If you have a qualifying child, attach Schedule EIC.	64a	Earned income credit (EIC)	64a	
	b	Nontaxable combat pay election	64b	
	65	Additional child tax credit. Attach Schedule 8812	65	
	66	American opportunity credit from Form 8863, line 8	66	
	67	Reserved	67	
	68	Amount paid with request for extension to file	68	
	69	Excess social security and tier 1 RRTA tax withheld	69	
	70	Credit for federal tax on fuels. Attach Form 4136	70	
	71	Credits from Form: a ☐ 2439 b ☐ Reserved c ☐ 8801 d ☐ 8885	71	
	72	Add lines 62, 63, 64a, and 65 through 71. These are your total payments ▶		72
Refund	73	If line 72 is more than line 61, subtract line 61 from line 72. This is the amount you overpaid		73
	74a	Amount of line 73 you want refunded to you. If Form 8888 is attached, check here ▶ ☐		74a
Direct deposit? See Instructions.	▶ b	Routing number	▶ c Type: ☐ Checking ☐ Savings	
	▶ d	Account number		
	75	Amount of line 73 you want applied to your 2013 estimated tax ▶	75	
Amount You Owe	76	Amount you owe. Subtract line 72 from line 61. For details on how to pay, see instructions ▶		76
	77	Estimated tax penalty (see instructions)	77	

Third Party Designee

Do you want to allow another person to discuss this return with the IRS (see instructions)? ☐ Yes. Complete below. ☐ No

| Designee's name ▶ | Phone no. ▶ | Personal identification number (PIN) ▶ | |

Sign Here

Under penalties of perjury, I declare that I have examined this return and accompanying schedules and statements, and to the best of my knowledge and belief, they are true, correct, and complete. Declaration of preparer (other than taxpayer) is based on all information of which preparer has any knowledge.

Joint return? See Instructions.
Keep a copy for your records.

| Your signature | Date | Your occupation | Daytime phone number |
| Spouse's signature. If a joint return, both must sign. | Date | Spouse's occupation | Identity Protection PIN (see inst.) |

Paid Preparer Use Only

Preparer's signature		Date	Check ☐ if self-employed	PTIN
Print/Type preparer's name				
Firm's name ▶			Firm's EIN ▶	
Firm's address ▶			Phone no.	

BEA

Form **1040** (2012)

Form **2106**	**Employee Business Expenses**	OMB No. 1545-0074
Department of the Treasury Internal Revenue Service (99)	► Attach to Form 1040 or Form 1040NR. ► Information about Form 2106 and its separate instructions is available at www.irs.gov/form2106.	**2012** Attachment Sequence No. **129**
Your name	Occupation in which you incurred expenses	Social security number

Part I   **Employee Business Expenses and Reimbursements**

Step 1 Enter Your Expenses		Column A Other Than Meals and Entertainment	Column B Meals and Entertainment
1 Vehicle expense from line 22 or line 29. (Rural mail carriers: See instructions.)	1		
2 Parking fees, tolls, and transportation, including train, bus, etc., that did not involve overnight travel or commuting to and from work	2		
3 Travel expense while away from home overnight, including lodging, airplane, car rental, etc. Do not include meals and entertainment	3		
4 Business expenses not included on lines 1 through 3. Do not include meals and entertainment	4		
5 Meals and entertainment expenses (see instructions)	5		
6 Total expenses. In Column A, add lines 1 through 4 and enter the result. In Column B, enter the amount from line 5	6		

Note: If you were not reimbursed for any expenses in Step 1, skip line 7 and enter the amount from line 6 on line 8.

Step 2 Enter Reimbursements Received From Your Employer for Expenses Listed in Step 1

7 Enter reimbursements received from your employer that were not reported to you in box 1 of Form W-2. Include any reimbursements reported under code "L" in box 12 of your Form W-2 (see instructions)	7		

Step 3 Figure Expenses To Deduct on Schedule A (Form 1040 or Form 1040NR)

8 Subtract line 7 from line 6. If zero or less, enter -0-. However, if line 7 is greater than line 6 in Column A, report the excess as income on Form 1040, line 7 (or on Form 1040NR, line 8)	8		
Note: If both columns of line 8 are zero, you cannot deduct employee business expenses. Stop here and attach Form 2106 to your return.			
9 In Column A, enter the amount from line 8. In Column B, multiply line 8 by 50% (.50). (Employees subject to Department of Transportation (DOT) hours of service limits: Multiply meal expenses incurred while away from home on business by 80% (.80) instead of 50%. For details, see instructions.)	9		

10 Add the amounts on line 9 of both columns and enter the total here. Also, enter the total on Schedule A (Form 1040), line 21 (or on Schedule A (Form 1040NR), line 7). (Armed Forces reservists, qualified performing artists, fee-basis state or local government officials, and individuals with disabilities: See the instructions for special rules on where to enter the total.) ► | 10 |

For Paperwork Reduction Act Notice, see your tax return instructions.   Form **2106** (2012)

EEA

Form **2106**

Department of the Treasury
Internal Revenue Service (99)

Your name

Employee Business Expenses

▶ Attach to Form 1040 or Form 1040NR.

▶ Information about Form 2106 and its separate instructions is available at www.irs.gov/form2106.

Occupation in which you incurred expenses

OMB No. 1545-0074

2012

Attachment
Sequence No. **129**

Social security number

Part I	**Employee Business Expenses and Reimbursements**		

Step 1 Enter Your Expenses

		Column A Other Than Meals and Entertainment	Column B Meals and Entertainment
1	Vehicle expense from line 22 or line 29. (Rural mail carriers: See instructions.) **1**		
2	Parking fees, tolls, and transportation, including train, bus, etc., that did not involve overnight travel or commuting to and from work **2**		
3	Travel expense while away from home overnight, including lodging, airplane, car rental, etc. Do not include meals and entertainment **3**		
4	Business expenses not included on lines 1 through 3. Do not include meals and entertainment **4**		
5	Meals and entertainment expenses (see instructions) **5**		
6	**Total expenses.** In Column A, add lines 1 through 4 and enter the result. In Column B, enter the amount from line 5 . . . . **6**		

Note: If you were not reimbursed for any expenses in Step 1, skip line 7 and enter the amount from line 6 on line 8.

Step 2 Enter Reimbursements Received From Your Employer for Expenses Listed in Step 1

7	Enter reimbursements received from your employer that were **not** reported to you in box 1 of Form W-2. Include any reimbursements reported under code "L" in box 12 of your Form W-2 (see instructions) **7**		

Step 3 Figure Expenses To Deduct on Schedule A (Form 1040 or Form 1040NR)

8	Subtract line 7 from line 6. If zero or less, enter -0-. However, if line 7 is greater than line 6 in Column A, report the excess as income on Form 1040, line 7 (or on Form 1040NR, line 8) **8**		
	Note: If both columns of line 8 are zero, you cannot deduct employee business expenses. Stop here and attach Form 2106 to your return.		
9	In Column A, enter the amount from line 8. In Column B, multiply line 8 by 50% (.50). (Employees subject to Department of Transportation (DOT) hours of service limits: Multiply meal expenses incurred while away from home on business by 80% (.80) instead of 50%. For details, see instructions.) **9**		
10	Add the amounts on line 9 of both columns and enter the total here. Also, enter the total on **Schedule A (Form 1040), line 21** (or on **Schedule A (Form 1040NR), line 7**). (Armed Forces reservists, qualified performing artists, fee-basis state or local government officials, and individuals with disabilities: See the instructions for special rules on where to enter the total.) . . . . ▶ **10**		

For Paperwork Reduction Act Notice, see your tax return instructions.

Form **2106** (2012)

BEA

			OMB No. 1545-0074
SCHEDULE A **(Form 1040)** Department of the Treasury Internal Revenue Service (99)	**Itemized Deductions** ▶ Information about Schedule A and its separate instructions is at www.irs.gov/form1040. ▶ Attach to Form 1040.		**2012** Attachment Sequence No. **07**

Name(s) shown on Form 1040 — Your social security number

Medical and Dental Expenses		Caution. Do not include expenses reimbursed or paid by others.			
	1	Medical and dental expenses (see instructions)	1		
	2	Enter amount from Form 1040, line 38 **2**			
	3	Multiply line 2 by 7.5% (.075)	3		
	4	Subtract line 3 from line 1. If line 3 is more than line 1, enter -0-		4	
Taxes You Paid	5	State and local (**check only one box**): a ☐ Income taxes, or b ☐ General sales taxes	5		
	6	Real estate taxes (see instructions)	6		
	7	Personal property taxes	7		
	8	Other taxes. List type and amount ▶	8		
	9	Add lines 5 through 8		9	
Interest You Paid **Note.** Your mortgage interest deduction may be limited (see instructions).	10	Home mortgage interest and points reported to you on Form 1098	10		
	11	Home mortgage interest not reported to you on Form 1098. If paid to the person from whom you bought the home, see instructions and show that person's name, identifying no., and address ▶	11		
	12	Points not reported to you on Form 1098. See instructions for special rules	12		
	13	Mortgage insurance premiums (see instructions)	13		
	14	Investment interest. Attach Form 4952 if required. (See instructions.)	14		
	15	Add lines 10 through 14		15	
Gifts to Charity If you made a gift and got a benefit for it, see instructions.	16	Gifts by cash or check. If you made any gift of $250 or more, see instructions	16		
	17	Other than by cash or check. If any gift of $250 or more, see instructions. You must attach Form 8283 if over $500	17		
	18	Carryover from prior year	18		
	19	Add lines 16 through 18		19	
Casualty and Theft Losses	20	Casualty or theft loss(es). Attach Form 4684. (See instructions.)		20	
Job Expenses and Certain Miscellaneous Deductions	21	Unreimbursed employee expenses - job travel, union dues, job education, etc. Attach Form 2106 or 2106-EZ if required. (See instr.) ▶	21		
	22	Tax preparation fees	22		
	23	Other expenses - investment, safe deposit box, etc. List type and amount ▶	23		
	24	Add lines 21 through 23	24		
	25	Enter amount from Form 1040, line 38 **25**			
	26	Multiply line 25 by 2% (.02)	26		
	27	Subtract line 26 from line 24. If line 26 is more than line 24, enter -0-		27	
Other Miscellaneous Deductions	28	Other - from list in instructions. List type and amount ▶		28	
Total Itemized Deductions	29	Add the amounts in the far right column for lines 4 through 28. Also, enter this amount on Form 1040, line 40		29	
	30	If you elect to itemize deductions even though they are less than your standard deduction, check here ▶ ☐			

For Paperwork Reduction Act Notice, see Form 1040 instructions.　　　Schedule A (Form 1040) 2012

EEA

SCHEDULE C (Form 1040)

Department of the Treasury
Internal Revenue Service (99)

Profit or Loss From Business
(Sole Proprietorship)

► For information on Schedule C and its instructions, go to www.irs.gov/schedulec.
► Attach to Form 1040, 1040NR, or 1041; partnerships generally must file Form 1065.

OMB No. 1545-0074

2012

Attachment
Sequence No. 09

Name of proprietor

Social security number (SSN)

A	Principal business or profession, including product or service (see instructions)	B	Enter code from instructions ►
C	Business name. If no separate business name, leave blank.	D	Employer ID number (EIN), (see instr.)

E Business address (including suite or room no.) ►
   City, state, and ZIP

F Accounting method: (1) ☐ Cash (2) ☐ Accrual (3) ☐ Other (specify) ►

G Did you "materially participate" in the operation of this business during 2012? If "No," see instructions for limit on losses . . . ☐ Yes ☐ No

H If you started or acquired this business during 2012, check here . . . . ►☐

I Did you make any payments in 2012 that would require you to file Form(s) 1099? (see instructions) . . . . ☐ Yes ☐ No

J If "Yes," did you or will you file required Forms 1099? . . . . ☐ Yes ☐ No

Part I Income

1	Gross receipts or sales. See instructions for line 1 and check the box if this income was reported to you on Form W-2 and the "Statutory employee" box on that form was checked . . . . ►☐	1	
2	Returns and allowances (see instructions)	2	
3	Subtract line 2 from line 1	3	
4	Cost of goods sold (from line 42)	4	
5	Gross profit. Subtract line 4 from line 3	5	
6	Other income, including federal and state gasoline or fuel tax credit or refund (see instructions)	6	
7	Gross income. Add lines 5 and 6 . . . . ►	7	

Part II Expenses Enter expenses for business use of your home only on line 30.

8	Advertising	8		18	Office expense (see instructions)	18
9	Car and truck expenses (see instructions)	9		19	Pension and profit-sharing plans	19
				20	Rent or lease (see instructions):	
10	Commissions and fees	10		a	Vehicles, machinery, and equipment .	20a
11	Contract labor (see instructions)	11		b	Other business property	20b
12	Depletion	12		21	Repairs and maintenance . . .	21
13	Depreciation and section 179 expense deduction (not included in Part III) (see instructions) . . .	13		22	Supplies (not included in Part III)	22
				23	Taxes and licenses	23
				24	Travel, meals, and entertainment:	
14	Employee benefit programs (other than on line 19) . . .	14		a	Travel	24a
				b	Deductible meals and entertainment (see instructions)	24b
15	Insurance (other than health) .	15		25	Utilities	25
16	Interest:			26	Wages (less employment credits)	26
a	Mortgage (paid to banks, etc.)	16a		27 a	Other expenses (from line 48)	27a
b	Other	16b		b	Reserved for future use . . .	27b
17	Legal and professional services	17				

28 Total expenses before expenses for business use of home. Add lines 8 through 27a . . . . . . ► | 28 |

29 Tentative profit or (loss). Subtract line 28 from line 7 . . . . | 29 |

30 Expenses for business use of your home. Attach Form 8829. Do not report such expenses elsewhere . . | 30 |

31 Net profit or (loss). Subtract line 30 from line 29.
   • If a profit, enter on both Form 1040, line 12 (or Form 1040NR, line 13) and on Schedule SE, line 2.
     (If you checked the box on line 1, see instructions). Estates and trusts, enter on Form 1041, line 3.
   • If a loss, you must go to line 32. | 31 |

32 If you have a loss, check the box that describes your investment in this activity (see instructions).
   • If you checked 32a, enter the loss on both Form 1040, line 12, (or Form 1040NR, line 13) and on Schedule SE, line 2. (If you checked the box on line 1, see the line 31 instructions). Estates and trusts, enter on Form 1041, line 3.
   • If you checked 32b, you must attach Form 6198. Your loss may be limited.

   32a ☐ All investment is at risk.
   32b ☐ Some investment is not at risk.

For Paperwork Reduction Act Notice, see your tax return instructions.

Schedule C (Form 1040) 2012

EEA

7. Sample Spreadsheet

Income & Expenses

	Ja	Feb	M	No	De	T
Income	70	700	750	0	400	335
Campsite						
Business	22	220	220	0	100	980
Telephone	0	0	0	25	0	25
Internet Svc	20	20	20	20	20	120
Postage	25	25	25	25	25	150
Parking &	0	0	0	0	0	46
Office Sup-	0	0	0	10	0	10
Repairs	25	5	10	0	35	75
Utilities	0	0	0	0	0	0
Electric						0
Gas						0
Water						0
						0
Total Ex-						0
Net Income	29	270	275	-80	180	140
	41	430	475	-80	220	194

8. Sample Auto Log

Date	Beg	End	Per	Bus	Tot	Purpose
1/1/13	15250	15260		10	10	Supplies
1/2/13	15260	15275		15	15	Customer
1/3/13	15275	15300	10	15	25	Customer
1/4/13						
1/5/13						

Resources

1.Workamper® News is a job-listing maga-zine that offers assistance in finding seasonal and temporary jobs. It also offers a support group for networking with other RVers who are also looking for seasonal, temporary work. They host a Rendezvous each fall for networking with other Workamping RVers.

Website: www.workamper.com

Mailing: Workamper® News Inc
110 Tulaka Blvd, Suite C
Heber Springs, AR 72543

2.Support *Your RV Lifestyle! An Insider's Guide to Working on the Road, 3rd ed.* by Jaimie Hall Bruzenak. Also, resume assis-tance, books, and articles about the RV life-style.

Websites: RVExperts.com,

RetiretoanRV.com

Email: calamityjaimie@gmail.com

Escapees RV Club is an organization dedicated to helping the RVer find support, knowledge, and parking for their RVs and the RV life style.

Website: www.escapees.com

Mailing: Escapees RV Club
101 Rainbow Drive
Livingston, Texas 77351

4. Terry Cooper, The RV Professor, teaches RV maintenance and repair. He teaches a class on RVDA, RVIA, and campground repair maintenance and certification.

Website: www.MobileRVAcademy.com

Email: Professor@MobileRVAcademy.com

Cell: 254-709-3251

5. Internal Revenue Service:

Website: www.irs.gov

Publication 529, Miscellaneous Deductions

Publication 463, Travel, Entertainment, Gift, and Car Expenses

<u>6. George M Montgomery, EA, author of this book.</u>

Tax consultation for individuals, small businesses, the self-employed and working RVers.

Website: BusinessAndTaxPlanning.com

RVTaxMaster.com

Email:
georgc@BusinessAndTaxPlanning.com

george@RVTaxMaster.com

Mail: George M Montgomery, EA
Business And Tax Planning
300 S Val Vista Drive, #118
Mesa, AZ 85204-1918

Index

2% Haircut, **113**

Adjusted Gross Income (AGI), **113**

Allowable Deductions, **47**, 49

auto insurance, 35

Auto Insurance, **33**

away from home, 51

Away-from-home expenses, **51**

Corporation, **83**

Deducting the RV, **61**

Domicile, **33**

Employee, **71**

Enrolled Agent, **13**

Form 2106 Employee Business Expense, **112**

Full-Time RVer, **58**

Health and XE "Health and Life Insurance" \b life insurance, 33

Health and Life Insurance, **33**

Home Base, **41**, **51**

How Long To Keep Documents, **99**

Independent Contractor, **71**

Itinerant Worker, **54**, **66**

Jaimie Hall Bruzenak, 50

Job Search Expenses, **48**, **95**

library card, 36

Limited Liability Company (LLC), **85**

mail-forwarding address, 54

Mail-Forwarding Service, **54**

Multiple Domiciles, **39**

Multi-State Returns, **105**

Non-Deductible Expenses, **57**

Non-Resident State, **106**

Office in the Home deduction, **68**

Partnership, **82**
Part-Time RVer, **58**
pension, 37
Record Keeping Systems, **88**
Renting Out The Home Base, 43
Resident State, **105**
resume, 50
S Corporation, **84**
Schedule C Income, **112**
search expenses, 50
Self-Employed, **72**
Self-Employment tax, **75, 112**
Single Member Limited Liability Company (SMLLC), **85**
Social Security Tax, **72**
Sole-Proprietorship, **81**
Standard Mileage Deduction, **94**
state of residency, 33
States without income tax, **107**
substantial break, 49
Tax Fraud, **102**
travel expenses, 48
Truck or Auto Registered, **35**
Vehicle Mileage Log, **93**
Vicinity Miles, **93**
Volunteer, **77**
Work and Travel Diary, **95**